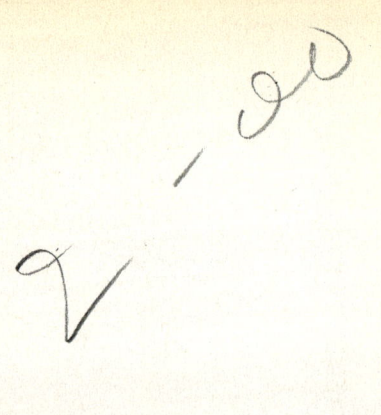

Glass, Mosaics and Plastics

Marshall Cavendish London & New York

Edited by Eric Shults

Published by Marshall Cavendish Books Limited
58 Old Compton Street
London W1V 5PA

© Marshall Cavendish Limited, 1975, 1976, 1977, 1979

This material was first published by Marshall Cavendish
Limited in the publication *The Encyclopedia of Crafts*

First printed in 1979

Printed in Great Britain
ISBN 0 85685 557 X

Introduction

Glass has long been valued for its qualities of transparency, reflection and refraction. As a material, it has been widely utilized and finished in a variety of ways for such diverse items as stained glass windows, mosaic murals, bowls and drinking vessels. More recently, plastic has appeared and, in certain forms, retains some of the qualities of glass. When the two materials are brought together, as in glass fibre, the result is a strong, resiliant and hard wearing material.

In *Glass, Mosaics and Plastics*, the beginner is shown, by means of step-by-step instructions accompanied by clear diagrams and attractive illustrations, how to complete a variety of projects using these materials in a wide range of forms. Whichever project you choose to begin with, the book presumes no previous knowledge and provides all information required to complete the job successfully. You can choose from a simple yet decorative painting on glass or, if you prefer practical items, make a leaded glass lampshade, glass fibre tray or screen, or a mosaic tabletop.

With the help of *Glass, Mosaics and Plastics*, you will be able to create useful and attractive articles for your home and friends gaining long lasting satisfaction from the knowledge that they have been made with your own hands.

Contents

Glass

Enlarging and Reducing designs

Glass is a familiar material which we use every day – for storage, drinking from, to let light into our homes and to look through. It can be stained, coloured, etched or engraved and craftsmen have produced exquisitely decorated pieces of glassware. As a material, it has the unique property of rigid transparency. Yet very few people attempt to work with it to produce decorative effects of their own. Reluctance to try handling glass may be explained by the mystique it has developed over the years – master craftsmen spend so long studying and learning how to make glass, to blow shapes and to master the arts of firing and annealing (the process of toughening glass). But there is no need to be overawed – with modern materials to help, you can easily learn to create decorative effects and to build up designs and structures in glass.

Enlarging and reducing designs

Whether you are using your own design or some pattern or illustration which you like, you will often need to enlarge or reduce it to the size you need. This is easy to do if you divide the design into small squares and divide the area it is to be transferred to into the same number of squares: you will find you can easily copy each square individually and so build up the whole design. You can reduce a design in just the same way, but copying on to smaller squares.

To avoid marking the original design, and to save the time it would take to draw lots of small squares, transfer the design on to graph paper. To do this, you can either trace it direct, if the graph paper is thin enough, or use tracing paper.

Trace the design on to tracing paper (fig.1). Lay this over graph paper. If you can see the squares clearly through the tracing paper, stick it down with clear tape, being careful that the tracing paper lies flat. If, however, you cannot see the squares clearly through the tracing paper, transfer the design to the graph paper either with carbon paper (dressmaker's carbon is fine) or by shading the back of the tracing paper with a soft pencil and drawing firmly over the design with a ballpoint.

Draw a rectangle to enclose the design (fig.2). This will be divided into a certain number of squares by the graph paper. If you are using plain paper instead of graph paper you must at this stage divide the rectangle by marking off each side and joining the marks to make a lot of small squares. It is helpful to number these for reference.

Next draw, preferably on tracing paper as before, a second rectangle, to the size you want the finished design to be and in the same proportions as the first one. Do this by tracing two adjacent sides of the first rectangle and the diagonal at which they meet. Extend them as far as required then draw in the other sides of the second rectangle (fig.3). Divide this into the same number of squares as the smaller one.

Carefully copy the design square by square. If you have to copy a flowing, curved line across several squares, mark the points at which it crosses the squares and then join them up in one flowing movement (fig.4).

1. *The design is traced on to graph paper or, alternatively, on to tracing paper which is then taped over the graph paper.*
2. *Enclose the design with a rectangle and number the squares.*
3. *The required size of the finished design is constructed on a second piece of paper and the same number of squares drawn on to it as appear in the original.*
4. *The design is enlarged by transferring the lines to the corresponding square on the larger rectangle.*

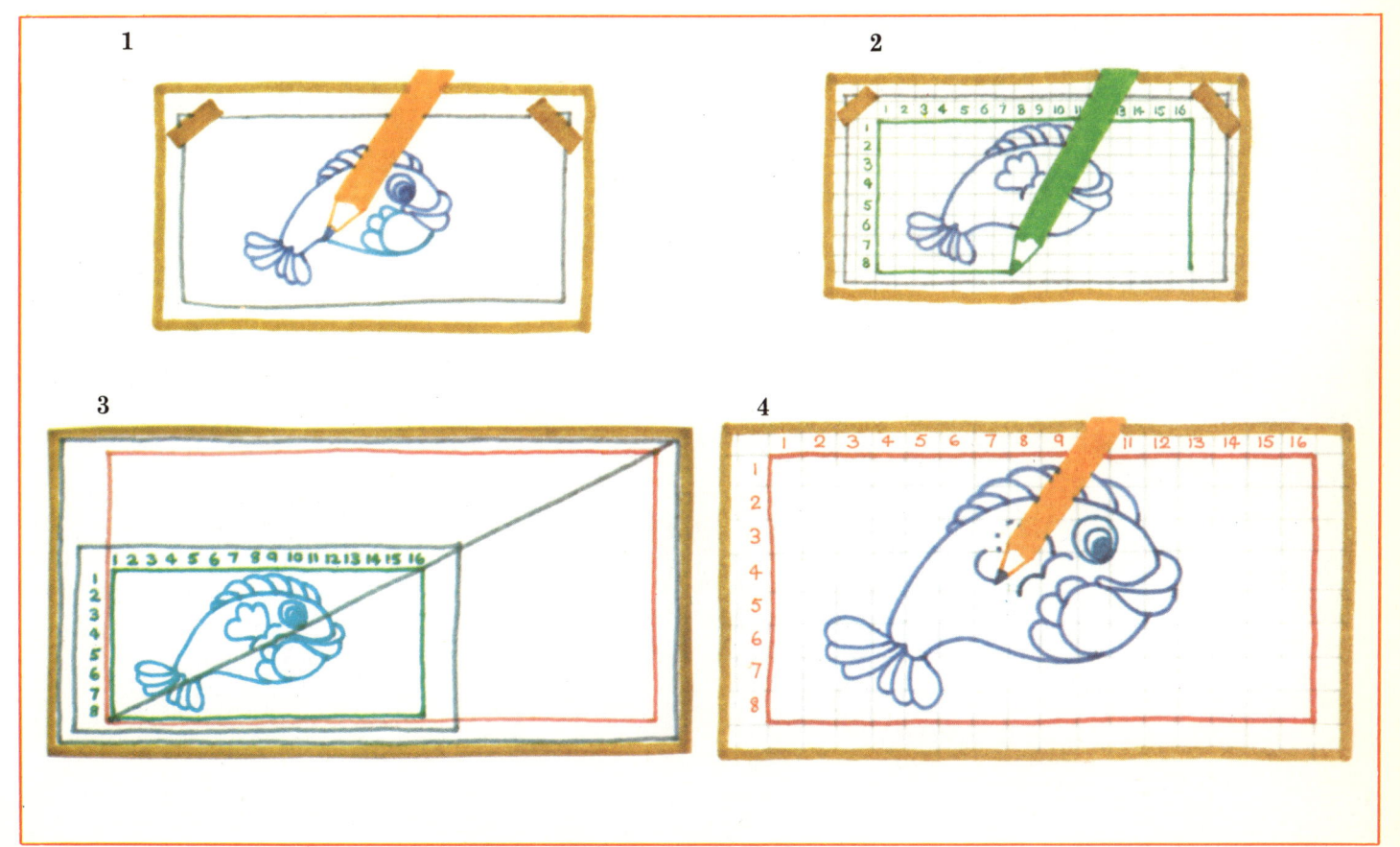

Painting on glass

The most attractive thing about glass as a medium for expression is its transparent quality – it is even more exciting to use if the glass is coloured. Painting on glass is one way to turn ordinary utensils, bottles and jars into more individual and attractive objects. It is also a means of re-cycling wine bottles, jam-jars and similar throw-away containers which can be converted with very little effort into canisters, vases for flowers, decorative cosmetic jars and ornaments.

Household items like glass ashtrays look very original with a design on the bottom or even covered entirely with paint. Drinking glasses can be personalized and inexpensive glass mixing bowls can be decorated to bring desserts and salads to the most elegant dinner table.

Many different shapes can be painted freehand on to glass and there are a number of other designs which can be used which require no drawing ability.

Marbled effect

A multi-coloured 'marbled' effect is easily obtained and can be made on the outside or, provided the top is broad enough, the inside of a container.

To marble the outside of a glass container, pour two or three colours on to a piece of cardboard and roll the bottle or jar in the paint. A wooden dowel or rod inserted in the container will help to roll it.

Allow the container to dry suspended over newspapers by a cord so that the excess paint drips off. This will add to the 'marbled' effect.

Marbling the inside of a container is even easier but remember that you need a fairly wide-mouthed container for the best results. Simply pour the paint into it as shown in fig.1 and revolve the container slowly. Pour out any excess paint and allow to dry.

Motifs may then be painted freehand on the outside, thus combining two techniques.

Tracing

Glass lends itself to this technique quite naturally. You simply tape a design to the inside of the glass and paint it on to the outside by following the lines. In this way, colourful scenes can be painted on drinking glasses or handsome silhouettes applied to glass vases.

If the container is too narrow to insert a paper pattern then the outline can be drawn on the exterior with a greasy pencil such as a chinagraph and filled in. The pencil marks can be rubbed off when the paint is dry.

Lettering is excellent for tracing from inside or out and kitchen canisters can be labelled in this manner.

Stick-on shapes

This is another versatile means of glass decoration. Self-adhesive labels are available from most art supply shops in the shape of circles, stars and rectangles and larger labels can be cut into any shape you wish.

Arrange the labels on the glass and then paint the glass surface. When the paint is dry, peel the labels off carefully. Stubborn or uneven edges can be evened up with a craft knife.

The tall yellow jar with blue circles was done in this way. The circles represent labels that have been removed. The inside has been painted with transparent blue paint.

Masking tape is useful for a number of designs and is indispensable for making clear, straight lines – a low-tack variety is recommended,

1. The inside of a jar may be marbled by pouring in several colours and revolving the jar before pouring out the excess colour.
2. To create a straight line masking tape is used. Make sure the edges are well pressed down.
Opposite: Backgammon board painted on the underside of a glass tabletop.

especially for taping over a previously painted area. The drinking glasses shown were decorated by masking off the area on either side of the desired stripes (fig.2) before painting them in. The graduation of the lines shown is another good decorative idea.

The multi-coloured 'hard edge' jar was also painted using masking tape.

You can experiment to get a rippled effect by putting on a very thin coat and waiting until it is sticky. Then dab on little dots of colour to give deliberately uneven colour.

Clean brushes thoroughly with white spirit or paint thinner, then wash in warm water and detergent. Rinse in cold water.

Paints sold for painting on glass are usually water-resistant so that the painted surface can be cleaned gently with cold water. Surfaces which receive constant washing are unlikely to retain their colour for any length of time so objects such as vases, window hangings or undersides of tabletops are really the best surfaces for glass painting. However, cheap drinking glasses and mixing bowls can be quickly decorated on the outside for the fun of it.

But for a more durable finish, especially if the glass will be in a steamy atmosphere, such as a kitchen or bathroom, coat the surface with a polyurethane clear varnish. Make sure the paint is completely dry before you apply this. The varnish will probably add a yellow tinge to the colours so test it on a scrap piece before using it.

Backgammon board
66cm (26in) by 33cm (13in).

You will need:
Graph paper and pencil.
Yellow, blue and red opaque paint (or your own choice).
Paint brush.
White spirit or paint thinner.
Low-tack masking tape.
Razor blade or craft knife.
Newspapers or old sheet.
Glass tabletop and frame or glass topped table.

Backgammon board

A backgammon board or chessboard can cover the entire surface of a small table or only the centre portion of a larger one such as a coffee table. Many shops sell glass-topped tables; but if you are having glass cut for a table frame or to cover a table, you should have the edges rounded to take off the sharpness and give a more 'finished' appearance.

The surface which you paint will be the underside of the glass and this will automatically protect it from abrasive cleaners, fluids and scratches. (Remember however that your finished design will be a mirror immage of the original drawing.)

Use graph paper to enlarge the design in fig.3a. For information on how to enlarge a design see 'Enlarging and reducing designs', page 6.

Protect working area with newspaper or an old sheet and clean the glass before beginning. Place the pattern on to a smooth flat working surface and put the glass on top of the pattern. If the edges are rounded put it bottom side up.

Mask off the border with masking tape (fig.3b) and paint the

border. Allow to dry thoroughly before proceeding further. Remove the tape carefully and clean up any unevenness in the painted lines with a razor blade or craft knife.

Mask off the blue triangles (fig.3c) and paint them. When dry, remove the tape with extra care since part of it has been placed over previously painted areas and there is always the danger of it pulling up some of the paint.

Mask off the red triangles (fig.3d); paint them and allow to dry before removing the tape.

Check the surface to make sure all is in order: you can remove odd flecks with a blade and touch up any gaps with a fine brush. Place the glass in position and you tabletop is complete.

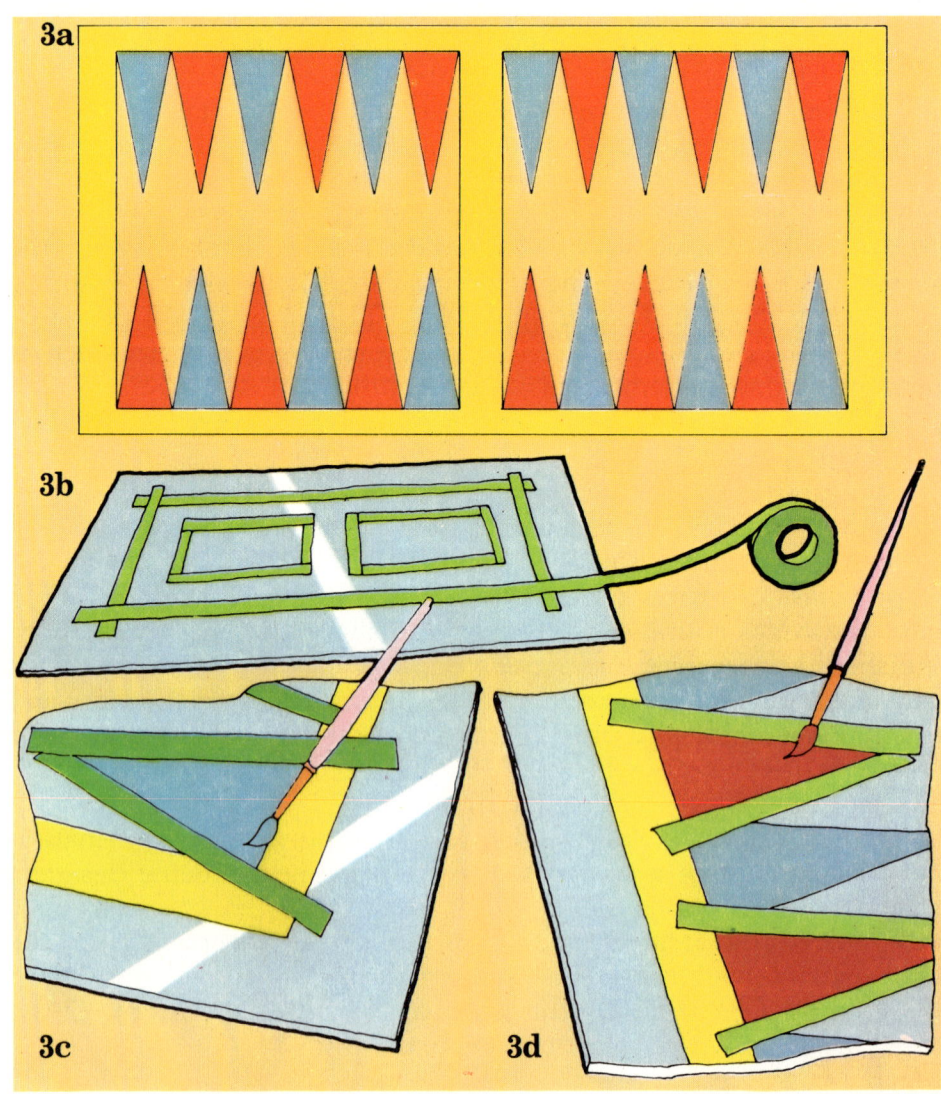

3a. The design for the backgammon board.
3b. The first stage of masking the glass for the backgammon board.
3c. The second stage. All the triangles of one colour are masked and painted at the same time.
The final stage. The alternate triangles are applied in a contrasting colour.

Stained glass effects

Traditional stained glass work involves using small pieces of differently coloured glass and joining them together with strips of lead. With transparent glass paints you can achieve a similar effect. There is also a type of leading which simulates the effect of traditional leading. This leading is in tube form like an oil paint, which is squeezed out where the lines are needed and takes an hour or so to harden.

When buying paint specify that it is to be used on glass. Craft shops and art supply shops stock transparent and opaque enamel paint which is designed especially for this purpose. Normally, this is oil based so you will need to buy white spirit or paint thinner for cleaning up. Inexpensive water colour brushes are perfectly suitable for this type of work but for especially intricate designs you should use a sable brush.

Thoroughly clean the glass to be decorated with warm water and detergent or soda. Alternatively, wipe clean with paint thinner or white spirit. If there is any grease on the surface the paint will not adhere properly. Rinse and dry the glass, taking care not to touch with your fingers the surface to be painted. Avoid resting your hand on the glass. If necessary, wear cotton gloves or put a piece of clean fabric under your hand to avoid getting grease from your skin on the surface.

Work in a reasonably dust-free room as dust and fluff will stick to the wet paint.

Mix the paint according to the manufacturer's instructions – some paints may only need to be shaken before application, others need to be shaken and then diluted with one part of water to two parts of paint. If the paint has to be mixed, be sure to get the proportions right – if the paint is too thick, it will be difficult to cover the glass evenly; if the paint is runny, it will tend to pull away from the edges and concentrate in the centre of each area of paint. When painting a flat surface keep the surface of the glass as level as possible to reduce the risk of the paint running. Apply the paint by letting it flow from the brush, rather than using vigorous brush strokes. If the paint is of the right consistency, it should level itself off into a smooth coat. The more paint you put on, the deeper the colour will be because less light is allowed through.

Let the paint dry for at least three hours before handling it or before putting another coat over it if you feel the colour needs to be deeper.

Painting and leading

Draw the design you want to paint on a piece of paper the same

Painting and leading
You will need : Glass. Transparent glass paints. Leading. Paint brush. White spirit or paint thinner. Paper and pencil. Four small blocks of wood, 13mm x 13mm ($\frac{1}{2}$in by $\frac{1}{2}$in) approx. Newspapers or old sheet. Polyurethane varnish (optional).

size as the finished object. You can make up your own design or copy an existing one: the most effective designs are usually made up of small segments. Too large an area of one colour means that you run the risk of the colour being uneven, although as you become more experienced, you may want to create a mottled effect. Lay down newspaper and thoroughly clean the glass. Place the design on a flat working surface and put the glass on top.

Check the manufacturer's instructions for the tube leading, which comes with a nozzle at the end of the tube. Cut the nozzle at different places to give different thicknesses – the nearer to the base the nozzle is cut the wider the hole will be and the thicker the line of leading. Make the first cut near the top of the nozzle; you can always cut again for a thicker line.

Trace the lines of the design with the leading. Hold the tube at a slight angle to the surface with the nozzle lightly touching the glass and squeeze gently and regularly as you draw the nozzle along the glass. After each line has been drawn, clean the nozzle with a pin before starting a new line. Be sure that the leading is free of holes and gaps and that it touches the glass right along its length. If you want the leading to lie flat, smooth it down gently with your fingers before it is quite dry – about 15 minutes after application. At this stage you can use a match-stick or spoon handle to push the leading over the glass to even out any irregularities.

Leave the leading to dry for an hour before starting to paint. Take the sheet of paper away from the glass. When using transparent paints it is important to be able to see right through the glass or it is impossible to judge how transparent the colours will look. White paper put down on your working surface will give a reflective background; the glass should be raised about 15mm ($\frac{1}{2}$in) above the paper by resting it on small blocks. Keep the surface of the glass level.

Paint the surface and allow to dry thoroughly.

Painting pictures on glass

Painting on glass is quite different from painting on a matt, opaque surface: the colour has a brilliant quality, it almost seems to glow. Transparent, rather than opaque, glass paints give the best effect. Detailed pictures can be painted on glass and can be combined with a silver foil backing.

Painting front surface

Choose a simple, decorative style with bold lines and colours such as 'The White Bird' illustrated here.

Clean the glass. Enlarge the graph pattern to the required size.

1 square = 2·5 cm (1") sq

Front surface

You will need:
Sheet of plate or window glass with
well-rounded edges. 'The White
Bird' is 20cm by 28cm (8in by 11in).
Transparent glass paints. 'The
White Bird' uses blue, green, red,
magenta and yellow.
Opaque enamel paint in white and
black or use opaque glass paints.
Water colour brushes, No. 2 and
No. 7.
Wooden 'bridge' for resting your
hand on when painting, 35cm by
5cm (14in by 2in) supported at
both ends by two small blocks.
White drawing paper.
White paper or cardboard.
Razor blade or craft knife.
Fine black felt-tip pen, pencil.
Old plate or piece of glass for a
palette.
Small brush, such as a pastry brush.
White spirit or paint thinner.
Lint-free paint rag (not paper
tissues).
Newspapers or old sheet.

For information on how to enlarge a design see 'Enlarging and reducing designs', page 6.

Place the glass over the drawing paper and run a pencil round it to get an accurate outline.

Trace a few guidelines with a felt-tip pen. Lay down newspaper. Mix up the paints if necessary on the palette, otherwise use straight from the jar. Place the glass over the white paper or card and start to paint. A 'bridge' is a useful tool preventing the hand smudging wet paint or making the glass greasy. It may be made very simply using a strip of wood with a small block at each end. Alternatively a strip of wood may be supported on two books. Resting your hand on the wooden bridge, start by painting in the background and then the fine detail, finishing off with the highlights in opaque white paint. Remember that the paint, once applied, cannot be worked over with a second coat until the first has dried (about four hours). Work quickly but carefully to avoid streaky lines.

Some clear areas of glass may look interesting. Try leaving a slim unpainted line around chosen areas of the design to highlight them or obtain a textured effect by scraping away some of the paint. Use the end of a paintbrush if the paint has not yet dried or a knife if it has.

You will probably find that you need to give two or sometimes

Above: The design for the White Bird is enlarged and transferred on to glass.

15

three coats of paint to the design. The extra paint adds depth and subtlety.

Mistakes can be rectified with a knife. If this is necessary, wait until the paint has dried and scrape off the accident zone. Then hold the glass on its edge and brush away the waste paint with a small, dry brush.

'The White Bird' has a mainly blue background which was painted first. One side was made darker by mixing blue, magenta and opaque black together. The bird is painted blue-green and opaque white feathers were added later. Other details and highlights are also painted in. Important shapes, such as the bird's head, are more heavily outlined.

Painting reverse surface

Having discovered how the glass paints handle you may like to try a more ambitious project using a technique popular in the nineteenth century. In this case the back of the glass is painted,

Reverse surface
You will need: Materials and tools as previously described. Cardboard. Clear adhesive. Kitchen foil.

Opposite top left: The first stage of the painting.
Opposite top right: The painting at a later stage, the bridge is used to prevent the design being smudged as the work progresses.
Opposite bottom: The completed painting.

Left: The design for the painting done on the reverse side of the glass.

Above: Two stages in the production of the painting.

the foreground first and the background last. Remember that the back of the painting will be a mirror image of the front, so that what is painted on the left-hand side of the picture will appear on the right-hand side of the finished painting. The glass is then backed with kitchen foil to give extra depth and sparkle as in 'The House' illustrated here.

Using the same materials and equipment as before draw a design on paper the same size as the glass, and trace over with felt-tip pen.

Lay down newspaper and place the cleaned glass, underside facing up, over the drawing and with a very fine brush and a little white paint diluted with white spirit or paint thinner trace a few guide-lines from the drawing. Keep the guidelines to a minimum other-wise they will show in the finished result. If you feel bold dispense with the guidelines altogether.

Keeping the drawing under the glass while painting, start by painting in the foreground. Remember that you are painting the back of the glass. The black lines of the sash windows in 'The House', for example, must be painted before the white curtains because they must appear in front. When the black lines are dry, paint in the white areas such as the curtains, fence, cloud edge and smoke. Aim for clear, decisive work as it is difficult to retrace your steps. Turn the glass over every now and again and examine the front of the painting to see whether everything is in the right

18

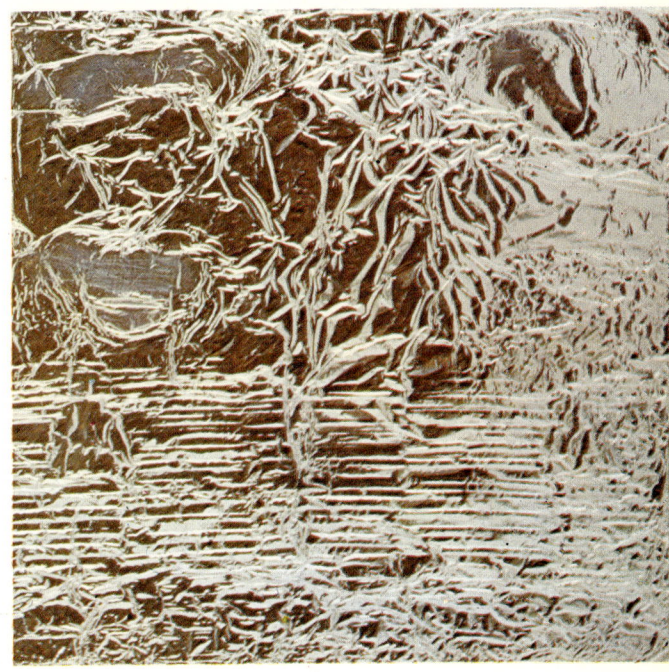

Above: The completed painting and the foil backing which has been crumpled to give the finished article added textural effect.

order. Where transparent colours are used, that is, everything except black and white, these are built up in successive layers. Remember that the backing foil will give extra sparkle when it is placed behind the paint. Leave strategic areas of the painting unpainted such as windows or the underside of clouds and these will then look silver. The foil is either used smooth or it can be crumpled to give an interesting texture. Working on the dull side press and ease the foil to obtain the desired effect; then check to see how it looks behind the painting and whether you have crumpled it in the right place, keep trying different effects with the foil so that you see how the picture changes.

When you are satisfied wrap the foil round a piece of cardboard the same size as the glass. Keep the shiny side outwards and overlap the foil at the back of the card. Stick down with adhesive. Turn the cardboard over and apply a speck of adhesive to each corner. Press the glass, painted side down, on to the backing and check that the edges are lined up.

Both types of painting can either be propped up against a window, wall or dresser and their appearance will be enhanced if they are framed. Use an ordinary picture frame for the painting with kitchen foil, but be sure to remove the backing to the frame for any other painting on glass. With the backing removed the light will be able to shine through the glass when it is hung in front of a window or other light source.

Decorative mirrors

<table>
<tr><td>

Cloud mirror

You will need:
Mirror.
Aerosol spray paint.
Masking tape.
Cups and lids.
Pencil and steel ruler.
Razor blade or craft knife.
White spirit or paint thinner.
Newspapers or old sheet.

</td></tr>
</table>

Painting designs on mirrors

Mirrors are used in interior decoration to emphasize space, to create atmosphere and to enhance and brighten dull corners of a room. They also make decorative, wipe-clean surfaces for tables, mats and borders round baths and basins which get spattered with water.

An ingenious way to ornament inexpensive mirrors and revamp old ones is to add colour to them. Any chips or flaws can be skilfully camouflaged.

'Do-it-yourself' shops sell sheet mirror glass and mirror mosaic squares. Sheet mirror should be bought no thinner than 4mm ($\frac{1}{8}$in) unless it is mounted on a solid backing. Most mirror suppliers will round the edges of glass on request to remove sharp edges. It is also possible to have a bevelled border round a mirror to give a finished look to the glass, however, this is rather more expensive. Mirror mosaic is normally available in squares, but oblong and other shapes are also available. The mosaic is bought in sheets on which many squares are mounted together and these must be pulled off and re-mounted for use individually.

Cloud mirror

A completely different technique has been used for the cloud mirror and by following the instructions given, you can reproduce it or create your own design. If you decide on the latter, choose a pattern which leaves a fair expanse of mirror uncovered so that it will remain functional. Old mirrors are perfectly suitable for this technique.

Clean the glass and cover the surface of the mirror with strips of masking tape.

The design shown was made by placing different-sized cups and lids – anything that will make a rounded edge would do – on the tape surface and tracing round them with a pencil to make a cloud outline. A ruler was used to mark the rain stripes.

When the design has been outlined cut round the pencil marks with a sharp blade taking care not to scratch the glass. For straight

Above: The completed cloud mirror. The technique can be adapted to suit any design you like.
Right: The mosaic mirror. The colour scheme can be chosen to suit the colour scheme of your room.

lines such as the rain stripes it is easier to draw the blade along a steel ruler. Do not use a wooden or plastic ruler as the blade is likely to cut the ruler and also spoil the work.

Remove the tape on the areas surrounding the design, leaving the shape of the design (the area not to be painted) still covered. In the case of the rain stripes every other stripe is peeled off.

The exposed areas can then be sprayed with aerosol spray paint in any colour and when dry the remaining tape removed, leaving the central shape clear and reflective.

It may be necessary to clean some of the edges with a razor blade to get a neat finish if the paint has seeped beneath the tape in any place.

Mosaic mirror

The small squares decorating the sheet mirror are each 2.5cm (1in) square. You can adapt the size of the design but you must be sure

Mosaic mirror
You will need: 200 mirror mosaic squares 2.5cm (1in) square. Mirror glass 35cm by 45cm (14in by 18in) and 3mm to 6mm ($\frac{1}{8}$in to $\frac{1}{4}$in) thick. Chipboard 19mm ($\frac{3}{4}$in) thick and the same dimensions as the mirror glass. Transparent glass paint in blue, yellow, red (mix the purple and green shades or buy ready-mixed). White spirit or paint thinner. Rubber based adhesive. Paint brush. Newspapers or old sheet. Attachments for hanging the mirror.

1. *The chipboard backing.*

it works out so that the squares will fit evenly into the given area. Begin by cleaning the glass. Experiment first on a few mosaic squares to test paint colour and strength. The purple and sea-green shades can be made by mixing red and blue and blue and green respectively.

When you are happy with the test samples both in colouring and degree of transparency proceed to paint the other squares, about 20 to 30 in each colour. The squares can be painted while still on the backing sheets and then removed when dry. Any remaining fibrous material must also be removed. Leave a few squares unpainted to give the finished design variety.

Before attaching the sheet mirror to the chipboard backing you must attach devices for hanging the mirror. When these have been secured to the back of the board, stick the glass and chipboard together (fig.1).

Stick the squares one by one to the front of the sheet mirror by applying a dab of glue to each one and pressing it down according to the design shown. Lay the tiles very close together. It does not matter if a little glue protrudes beyond a square since the next one will cover it. Otherwise wipe with a damp cloth. When the squares on the front have had time to set, apply a row around the side edges of the mirror to finish. Polish with a slightly damp cloth and the mirror is ready to mount on the wall.

Reflecting cocktail mats

The cocktail mats were made using an improvised mirror of plastic foil as the reflective surface.

Enlarge the pattern given (fig.2a) so that the outside length measures 5cm (2in) and trace it on to paper. (In fig.2c the purple area represents the pattern lines and, if you prefer, a heavy cardboard template like the one shown can be used.)

On the underside or unbevelled side of the mats, cover the opposite corners on each with overlapping strips of masking tape so that an area slightly larger than the pattern is covered (fig.2b). Place the pattern over the tape so that it is aligned correctly and the outside of the first line of the design is about 4mm ($\frac{1}{4}$in) from the outside edge of the glass. Then, with a sharp blade cut round the edges of the pattern (fig.2c). If you are using a paper pattern simply mark off the areas of the pattern with a pencil and cut by placing a ruler along the line.

When the corners have been cut out, remove all the tape except that of the design. Lay down newspaper, clean the glass and paint over the entire undersurface of each mat.

Paint the plywood baseboards in the same colour and allow to

Above: The completed cocktail mats.

22

dry: paint both sides and edges unless you intend to apply a felt backing.

Carefully remove the rest of the tape. Be sure that the paint seals are broken with a blade first so that you do not pull up any of the paint with the tape. Clean any uneven edges of the design with a knife. The pattern areas remain transparent.

Cut out 8 triangles of foil, each large enough to cover the design area. Smooth the triangles flat and tape them in place over the paint with pieces of masking tape so that all the transparent or unpainted areas become reflective.

Spread a thin layer of adhesive on the undersurface of the glass including the foil and masking tape and spread another layer on the baseboards. Then join them together (fig.2d).

Felt may be glued to the underside to protect table surfaces from scratching.

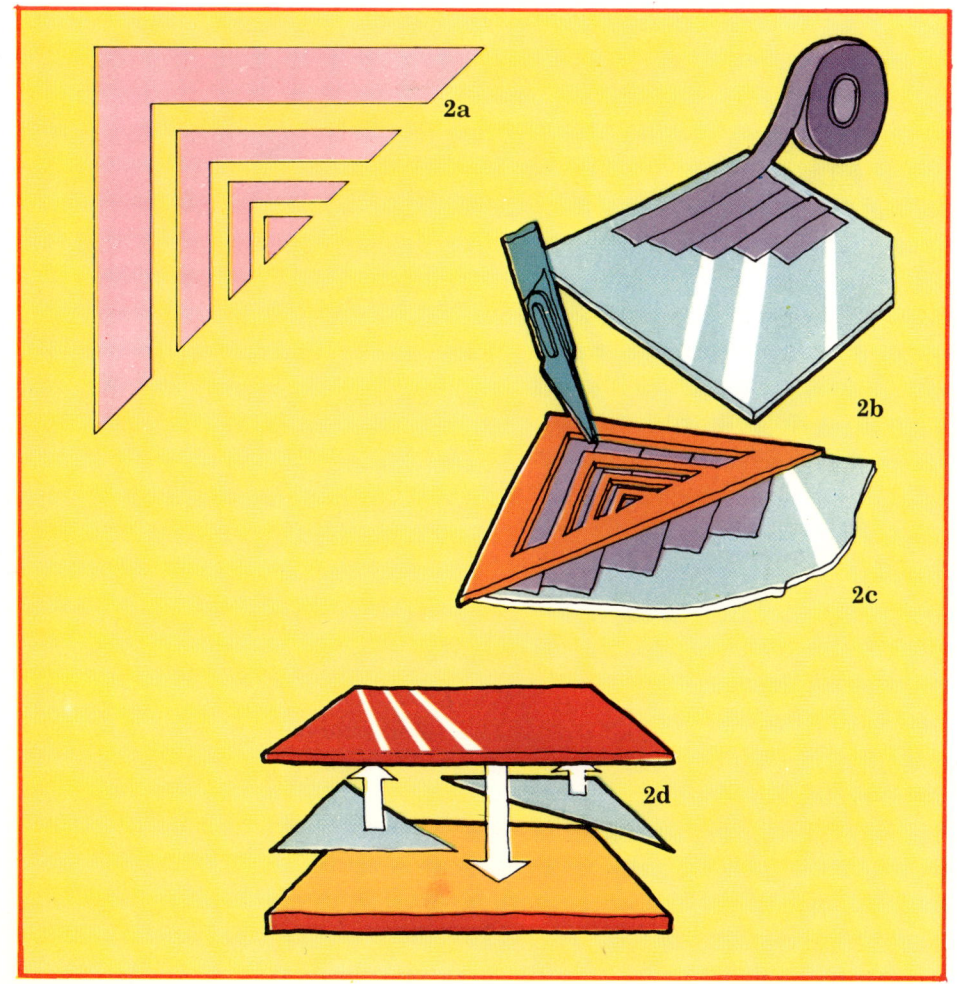

2a. Enlarge the pattern for the template and cut from a piece of card.

2b. Stick masking tape to the corners of the glass making sure that the area covered is larger than the design.

2c. Using the card template, cut the design into the tape and remove the waste.

2d. After painting, remove the tape and glue the glass, foil and plywood together.

23

Etching glass

Etching techniques

Etching on glass, allowing controlled amounts of acid to eat away selected parts of the glass surface to make a design, is an old-established craft. It dates from the discovery, in 1771, of hydrofluoric acid. This acid is very dangerous and should not be used in the home.

Be sure only to buy etching fluid which has sodium fluoride as its active ingredient. Other etching fluids containing hydrochloric acid or ammonium fluoride can cause burns or poisoning. Sodium fluoride, however, only attacks glass and can be used quite safely in the home provided the manufacturer's instructions are carefully followed.

Sodium fluoride etching fluid produces a frosted effect. It can be bought as part of a kit, which includes all you need to start decorative etching – gum-backed stencils, applicators and tweezers as well as etching fluid. The individual components are also available separately at art and craft shops.

Any glass may be used for etching. The finest decorative work is usually done on lead glass, because it is relatively soft and very clear. Most glass in the home is likely to be a variety of soda-lime-silica glass which, as the name implies, is largely made of these three constituents – silica sand, soda ash and limestone. This glass has a tendency to be greenish, like old bottles, and small quantities of other chemicals are usually added to reduce this.

It is not necessary to insist on using lead glass for your decorations – you will be much better advised to use objects you can find around the home or buy cheaply. Delightful effects may be created on old jam jars or coffee containers, easily bought spice jars or cheap wine glasses. All of these will probably be made of soda-lime-silica glass.

Within this broad category, there are hundreds of different types of glass, with slightly different constituents and properties. Etching fluid will react slightly differently on each of them, so you will have to experiment, particularly with the etching time. It is advisable, also, to make your first attempts on waste pieces of

Opposite: Glassware attractively decorated using the etching techniques described here.

glass until you are confident in your own ability.

To achieve a good pattern it is absolutely essential that you control the application of the acid carefully and accurately. This is done by 'stopping-out'. There are a variety of materials you can use for this which will prevent the acid from reaching the areas you want to remain unaffected. A glass-etching kit will supply gum-backed stencils or you could use glue and paper, the best material, however, is a contact plastic. The essential points are that the material should be resistant to the acid and that there should be no bubbles or unglued parts along the edge, under which the acid might seep to spoil the line. When you have stuck the material down, rub it with the back of a spoon or, better still, with a small roller to smooth down the edge.

If you are using ready-made, gum-backed stencils, this will be no problem. Simply cut the appropriate section from a stencil sheet, peel off the backing and stick it on. If you are using several pieces – as for lettering – make sure they are aligned properly.

1. For lettering, the stencils are cut from contact plastic before sticking to the glass. Right: The finished result.

If you are not using ready-made stencils, it will be necessary to cut the design from the stop-out material. It is easiest to work if you can fit the design on to one piece of stop-out material so that it can be cut and handled as one piece. This is possible if you are working on flat glass or straight-sided tumblers or jars. In this case you can draw the design on to the material and cut it out before attaching it to the glass (fig.1). You can use ordinary stencils, or trace a design you like, or draw your own. Until you cut the design out, you can keep altering and improving it.

A word of warning: with some patterns and letters, you will have to stop-out the inside as well as the outside of the shape although they do not connect. For example, to etch the letter 'O', it is important that the centre piece of stop-out material be positioned exactly in the middle of the shape. In such cases it is best to stick a solid piece of material on the glass, with the letter drawn on it and then cut out and lift off the area you want to etch, using a razor blade or a sharp knife and tweezers.

If you are working with glass that is curved in two directions – like a wine glass, as opposed to a straight-sided tumbler – you will not be able to lay a flat sheet on it without it creasing, unless it is a very small area which requires etching. To overcome this problem, cut the material into strips before drawing the design. After preparing the glass (see 'Etching method', below), stick the strips on to the glass to cover the area to be etched (fig.2) and draw the design in pencil. When you are satisfied with it, cut the material carefully with a scalpel or sharp knife and lift off the parts covering the areas to be etched.

Etching method

Clean the glass using methylated spirit or white spirit followed by warm soapy water and dry thoroughly. It is important to remove all grease from the surface as the fluid will not act properly on a greasy surface. Be careful not to get finger-marks on the clean glass. Handle it only by areas that will not be etched.

Prepare your stop-out stencil. Using tweezers to avoid finger-marks, put the stencil in position on the glass. If you are working on curved glass, now is the time to cut the stencil. If you are using more than one piece of stop-out material, then be careful to align them accurately. Smooth the material down with a spoon or small roller to make sure that the edges are solid. This is particularly important if you have overlapping pieces, for the join may be a vulnerable point.

It is advisable to leave the stop-out stencils for an hour or two after they are stuck down, to set firmer. It is much more important

Etching
You will need:
Glass.
Etching fluid (sodium flouride-based).
Stop-out material.
Brush, or absorbent cotton swabs on sticks.
Tweezers.
Spoon or small roller.
White spirit or paint thinner.
Razor blade or craft knife.
Pencil.
Newspaper or old sheet.

to get a good edge than to be able to peel the material off easily. Most adhesives, even contact adhesives, set harder if left for a while and so will resist the acid better.

Lay down newspaper. Make sure the surface to be etched is horizontal, as the etching fluid will run down a slope. If you are working on a curved surface, such as a jar or drinking glass, you will have to etch it a bit at a time. Keep the part you are etching horizontal by holding it in place with book-ends, paperweights or anything to stop it rolling.

Take the container of etching fluid and check the manufacturer's instructions. They will probably tell you to shake it vigorously to dispel any sediment that may have gathered, which would leave a diluted and ineffective solution at the top. Use a small brush or a swab of absorbent cotton on the end of a toothpick to paint the fluid on to the glass. Put it on as thick as you can without spilling it. Leave the fluid on the glass for 5 to 10 minutes. The exact length of time needed for the fluid to work will depend on the glass: experience is the only real guide.

Wash off the fluid with warm running water. Do this quickly and carefully to avoid dislodging the stop-out material. Dab the glass dry with a clean cloth and take a good look at it. If there are any patchy areas where the fluid has not worked properly, make sure the glass is completely dry and re-apply the fluid.

If you are working on a curved surface and the section you have been working on is completed, turn the glass, prop it up again and apply the fluid to the next area.

When all the unmasked areas in your design have been frosted, peel off the stencils. If they are stuck very hard, try soaking them in warm water. In really intractable cases, try using lighter fluid to loosen the glue.

2a. The glass is covered with strips of contact plastic.
2b. Draw the design on to the plastic.
2c. Carefully cut the design from the stop-out material and make sure all the edges are pressed down firmly.

Engraving glass

The art of engraving

Engraving can be as simple or as skilled as you like, from straight
forward initials cut into a drinking glass to intricate designs on
panels or bowls. Either way it is a beautiful medium and simple
projects require only a little patience and practice. Engraving is a
technique of cutting into a hard surface, in this case glass, and has
been practised since at least the eighteenth century. Nowadays,
there are two different methods of glass engraving – wheel and
point work. Wheel engraving is the grinding into the surface of a
piece of glass using small copper discs and an abrasive cutting
agent such as Carborundum grit, or you can use a proprietary
abrasive wheel. Point work, on the other hand, depends for its
effect upon marking the surface with a diamond or steel point.
The point is held in an electric vibro-engraver which makes the
craftsman's work a lot easier.

Point work is either the drawing of fine lines into the surface of
the glass or the creation of thousands of fine dots. These are made
by gently striking the surface of the glass with the point; this
technique is called 'stippling'. Point work relies for its effect on the
contrast between light and dark. A cut shows white against the
uncut areas of glass which appear as a dark background.

For wheel engraving there are many different shapes of wheel:
cone, pencil and tapered wheels and wheels with flat or rounded
edges.

Most types of glass can be used for engraving, but some are much
better than others. Probably the best type of all is soft lead glass.
Of this kind, the most satisfactory to work with is English full
lead crystal containing over 30% lead oxide. This type of glass –
sometimes known as flint glass – is not only 'gentle' enough for
fine work but, due to its clarity and high refractive qualities, will
make any engraving work show up more brightly.

Window glass, although it can be used, is not very suitable for
engraving. It is extremely hard and will very soon blunt the steel
engraving points. For engraving large panels of window glass use a
diamond point. Most glass objects found in the home such as

1. A piece of dowel is used to hold the engraving point for sharpening.

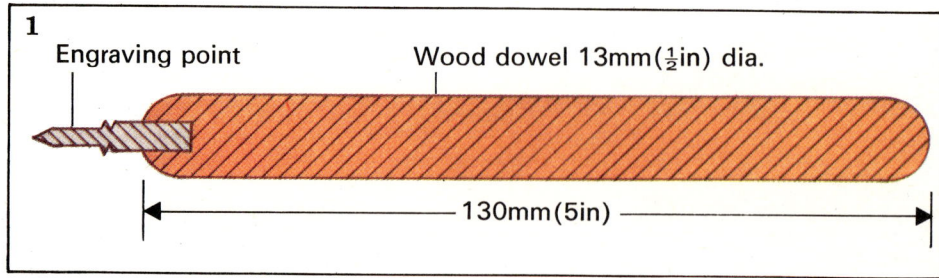

1

Engraving point   Wood dowel 13mm($\frac{1}{2}$in) dia.

←———————— 130mm(5in) ————————→

cheap bottles and jars are too hard for satisfactory engraving.
The key to the success of any glass engraving work is the steel point. Unless the tungsten-carbide tip is kept to a needle point sharpness, it will be useless for doing fine work. A slight flatness on a tip will probably bounce off the surface of the glass without leaving a mark. Worse still, such a point could easily chip the glass and shatter it.
By using an abrasive wheel of suitable material for sharpening tungsten-carbide the engraving point can be sharpened as you hold it in a piece of dowel rod (fig.1). Rotate the rod between the fingers and move the point across the wheel at a low angle. Since the tip is extremely hard it will not be easy to sharpen. A jeweler's eyepiece with a x4 magnification or more will enable you to check the point accurately.

Engraving a tumbler

Engraving a tumbler or wine glass is both uncomplicated and satisfying. First, make a detailed drawing of the design. Remember that the finished product will be in black and white. A good and carefully prepared drawing will lead to a better engraving.
Clean the glass with paint thinner or white spirit.
Tape the lettering or design to the inside of the glass with small pieces of clear tape. Make sure the pattern is correctly positioned before starting to engrave. Once a cut has been started it cannot be removed.
Put on the goggles and put the cloth over your knees. The cloth cuts out glare from the light. Cradle the glass on the knees and adjust the lamp (which stands on the floor) so that it shines horizontally into the glass.
Turn the vibro-control on the electric engraver to a very fine setting. Hold the engraver as upright and as near to a right angle to the glass as possible (fig.2). Hold the engraver in the same way as you would hold a pen.
Gently strike the surface of the glass with the engraving point. For solid parts of the design (such as lettering), outline the shape first

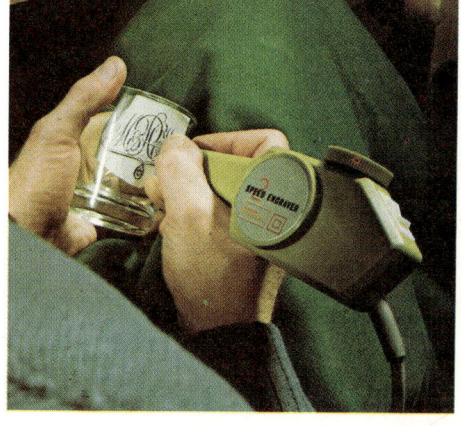

Above left: A glass tumbler is a good project for a first attempt at engraving.
Above: The method of holding the glass and vibro-engraver. The design is taped inside the glass.

with a single line. Remove the paper pattern and do the in-filling with either dots or lines. The more dots and lines there are, the whiter will the design appear. Any shading can be done by skating the point across the glass, much as a pencil is used for sketching. To achieve even finer markings the engraving point can be used in the sharpening holder. The method is the same as with the electric vibro-engraver but at a greatly reduced speed.

If the design goes all the way round the glass insert a piece of black paper into the glass. This will help you to focus on the lines at the front without the distraction of lines showing through from the other side.

Lines made by the vibro-engraver will be no more than a few hundreths of a millimetre deep and will easily collect dirt and grease from the hands. An occasional wipe with paint thinner or white spirit will soon remove this making the engraving clean and visible once more.

If, while engraving, you hear a slight ringing sound it is likely that your point is blunt. If the glass whirs, it is probably too thin and the point will rebound. You can help to overcome this problem by holding the glass firmly while engraving. Should this fail to solve the problem, a slight increase in the depth of cut may well be the answer. Remember, however, that this will also mean extra 'hammering' on the glass, which could all too easily result in the glass cracking.

If you do crack the glass, do not immediately assume that it is a result of your own carelessness. Often, glass will crack for no apparent reason. This is unfortunate, but is usually due to the stresses and strains put upon the glass during manufacture, which are only released when the glass is actually pierced. Glass also becomes brittle with age. Cracking can even occur some hours after engraving work has been completed. One of the hazards of engraving work is the risk that many hours of patient work may eventually shatter. Do not let the same thing happen to your enthusiasm as shattering only occurs in one or two cases in a hundred.

After you have mastered the basic skill of engraving on one or two simple projects, try a more demanding piece such as a panel like the one shown here. Lay down a dark-coloured blanket, thick cloth or felt underlay and tape glass over the design (fig.2). Using the vibro-engraver, score the outline of the design (fig.3). If the vibro-engraver begins to get heavy, support it by wrapping it with masking tape and suspend it from the ceiling with an elastic luggage support (the type which wraps around a luggage rack). Fill in the detail of the design as previously described. The sky and grass are engraved with a wheel which is always used for large areas of shading. Hold the grinder in one hand supported by the other, and move the grinder across the glass in even strokes. While grinding, always wear a mask to keep out the dust.

Right: The glass is taped over the design before following the outline with the vibro-engraver.

Bottle chopping

What a waste it is that so many good-looking bottles are non-returnable and often seem destined for the waste bin once they are empty. And yet think how many things you could make from

Below: Old bottles and jars can be cut to create useful items such as vases, storage jars and ashtray.

bottles if you could slice them. The bottoms of bottles make ashtrays; a bottle with just the top cut off makes a vase; stubby bottles can be corked and made into storage jars; Chianti bottles convert into hanging baskets – your imagination is the only limitation. You should not, however, attempt to make drinking glasses, the edge, after grinding, may contain glass dust and this can be lethal if ingested.

The method for cutting bottles is very simple, and the raw materials, once you have a cutter, are free. Any bottles will do. Virtually all wine bottles are non-returnable, and some of them are extremely handsome; many soft drinks and some beers come in non-returnable bottles. You can use your own, or try asking a restaurant or bar if they have bottles to spare; they will probably be glad to get rid of empties.

The only essential tool is an adapted glass cutter. A glass cutter does not actually cut glass itself; rather, it marks a score line along a sheet of glass, which weakens the glass along that line. When you put stress on the glass (with sheet glass, usually by bending it), the glass fractures along the line.

The score line is made by a small wheel with a sharp edge which is drawn, quite gently, along the glass. The tip of wheel can be made of industrial diamonds, which will last practically forever, or of toughened steel. Steel ones are much cheaper and quite adequate for home use – one wheel should mark a hundred bottles and replacements cost next to nothing.

The cutter to be used on bottles has to be adapted to make sure you can draw a regular line around a bottle. You could rig up a gadget yourself with an ordinary glass cutter, or you can buy a kit with the appropriate cutting tool from art and craft shops.

Bottle chopping

You will need:
Bottle.
Bottle chopper.
Silicon carbide paper.
Goggles.
Rubber gloves.
Newspaper.

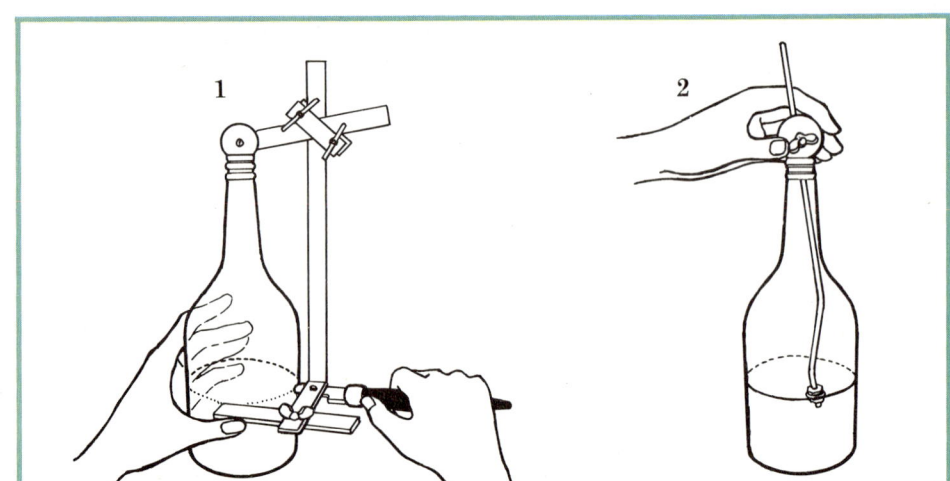

1. *Rotate the bottle and score the glass with the wheel of the cutter.*
2. *Tap gently along the score line with the tapper inserted in the bottle.*

The manufactured brands use various techniques to position the cutter. Some involve laying the bottle on its side over a vertical cutter; others provide a base and vertical pole with which to position the cutter.

The cutter shown (fig.1) works by suspending the cutter, via a pair of metal rods in a cross shape, from the top of the bottle. The two rods are clamped together and, by loosening the clamp and adjusting the rods, you can position the cutter so that it is horizontal and exactly where you want to cut the bottle. A guide bar is fitted next to the cutter to help keep it in position as you rotate the bottle.

This technique is easiest on straight-sided, round bottles. Start with a couple of bottles of no great interest, till you have mastered the knack. Before cutting, soak off any labels, as they will interfere with the cutting wheel, also, clean the bottle.

Fix the bottle chopper in position so that the cutter is horizontal and just touching the bottle. Press both cutter and guide bar gently against the bottle and slowly turn the bottle. Don't press hard or you will get a messy break and wear out the wheel quicker. There should be a barely audible scraping sound as you turn the bottle and a very thin score mark where the cutter has been.

Carefully turn the bottle around once. Make each movement as long as possible to minimize stopping and starting. Do not go over any part of the score line twice but make sure that the line is continuous. As soon as it is, this stage is done – with practice, it only takes a matter of seconds.

There are two methods by which you can put stress on the glass and make it fracture along the score line: using a tapper, or using hot and cold water.

To use a tapper, insert a small hammer (provided by the manufacturers of bottle choppers) into the bottle and tap gently along the score line, from the inside, till it breaks.

The tapper must be adjusted so that it is positioned exactly level with the score-line. It is held in place by washers at the top of the bottle (fig.2). Force is quite unnecessary, a few soft taps at the same place will produce a visible crack. Then tap all round the bottle, tapping about 13mm ($\frac{1}{2}$in) ahead of the crack, until the crack goes all the way round. If the bottle does not separate, look to see where the crack is not complete and tap there again.

For some bottles, especially odd-shaped ones, you will not be able to touch the score line with the tapper. For these, use the other method.

Using hot and cold water involves a little more care and patience than the tapping method but will produce a cleaner break and can be used at times when the tapper is impractical to use.

Fill the bottle with hot but not boiling water – adding a cup of cold water to recently boiled water should do. Leave it to stand for a minute, so that the water warms the glass from the inside. Then rotate the bottle underneath the cold tap, with the water running along the score line as much as possible. Hold both top and bottom of the bottle firmly while you do this. It will probably not separate first time, but you should see a crack mark appearing, especially if the glass is thick. If the water in the bottle is still hot, top it up if necessary, let it stand again and then repeat the process. If the water has cooled, repeat the process from scratch. Only trial and error will tell you just how hot the water should be and how careful you have to be with the bottle. Always hold it as close to the bottom of the sink as possible to minimize the risk of fragments of glass ricocheting dangerously. This is unlikely as the glass will almost certainly break along the score line but if you are not prepared for this, the sudden break may surprise you into dropping the bottle.

However clean your break, there will be rough edges and you must smooth these down before using the glass objects. Do this with wet and dry silicon carbide paper available from most hardware stores.

The paper is best used with a little water. Use a coarse grade first and then smooth with a finer grade. Finish the glass over newspaper, carefully wrap up the newspaper before throwing away. Careful finishing is essential as jagged edges can be dangerous. Remember, do not drink from a cut bottle just in case there are grains of glass in what seems to be a smooth surface.

Square and oval bottles are more tricky than round bottles as the method given will not give you a horizontal cut. Because of the shape of the bottle, you will get a curved cut. This can look very attractive, it does, however, mean that the stress line will be irregular and you may not get a good break – but the principles are the same. It's just a little more tricky to break and smooth the bottles accurately but the results can be well worth it. Use your imagination and try cutting a bottle you like for what ever use you think it may be suitable. You will be surprised at the number of uses to which cut bottles and jars can be put.

Once you have cut a few, and mastered the techniques involved, you will be able to cut a bottle for any purpose as and when it is needed. Always remember though, that glass powder can be dangerous and must never be ingested; this can not be emphasised too strongly. Never use a cut bottle as a drinking vessel or to hold food.

Animals
from glass rod

Working with glass rod

Glass will soften if it is subjected to sufficiently high temperatures. By heating glass rods over a blowtorch until they become pliable, the rods can be formed into a wide variety of objects such as animals, flowers, jewelry and Christmas decorations. This chapter explains the basic techniques of modelling with glass rods and shows you how to make two simple objects – a dachshund and a swan. Once you have become proficient in the techniques you can go on to more ambitious projects.

Glass rods come in many different colours, both clear and opaque. The glass rods used here are made of soda lime which has a low melting point – about 530°C (1000°F) – but other types are available.

Glass rods are supplied in lengths of 7.5cm to 30.5cm (3in to 12in). A number of different diameters are available but the most useful for making glass animals are 3mm to 9mm ($\frac{1}{8}$in to $\frac{3}{8}$in).

Glass jars and bottles provide another supply of glass which is readily available and does not cost anything. These can be broken up and used: place the bottle or jar on a hard surface, wrap in a

Below: Attractive animals made from glass rod using the techniques described here.

37

rag or several sheets of newspaper to prevent splinters flying out and smash with a hammer. The pieces of glass can be left in their original shape and embellishments added. For example, an appropriately shaped piece of glass could be turned into a fish by softening the sharp edges and adding blobs of glass, for eyes and mouth, by the methods described here.

Because melting glass is a potentially dangerous occupation, it is essential that you should learn the correct way of working. Make sure that your chair is comfortable and the correct height for your working surface. The elbows should rest on the surface with the hands in easy reach of the flame. Make sure your working area is well ventilated.

There are a number of different types of blowtorch that can be used for making glass animals. The professional uses a torch which runs on gas and compressed air. These are complicated to use but necessary for detailed work. For making simple glass animals a blowtorch which runs on gas alone is adequate. This torch consists of a flame nozzle, a length of rubber tubing, a valve to control the flow of gas and a gas cylinder. The blowtorch is assembled as shown in fig.1. When the blowtorch is ready to use, the gas is turned on and the flame is lit with a match. The flame has a bright blue cone-shaped centre surrounded by a paler blue flame. The hottest part of the flame is at the tip of the bright blue cone, and this is where the glass is held for melting. Inside this blue cone is an area of unburnt gas which is not as hot and will not melt the glass as quickly. The coolest part of the flame is at the tip of the paler blue flame and the glass is held here for pre-heating and cooling. Always turn out the flame when you have finished using it – never leave a flame burning unattended.

Glass is a poor heat conductor and the rods can be held about 5cm (2in) away from that part which is in the flame without burning your hands.

For a right-handed person, the main weight of glass is usually supported in the left hand, leaving the right hand free to manipulate the glass or to hold a secondary piece for joining. The left hand is cupped over the glass rod which is supported on the fingertips. The right hand is generally held palm up, and the glass rod is supported by the fingertips (fig.2). By holding the glass rods in this way, it is possible to roll them backwards and forwards in the flame so that the glass will melt evenly. When working with very small pieces of glass the hand positions must be modified. Glass rods should be rolled backwards and forwards in the flame for even heating. If a rod is held still in the flame, one side will melt quicker than the other. It takes about 30 seconds to a minute

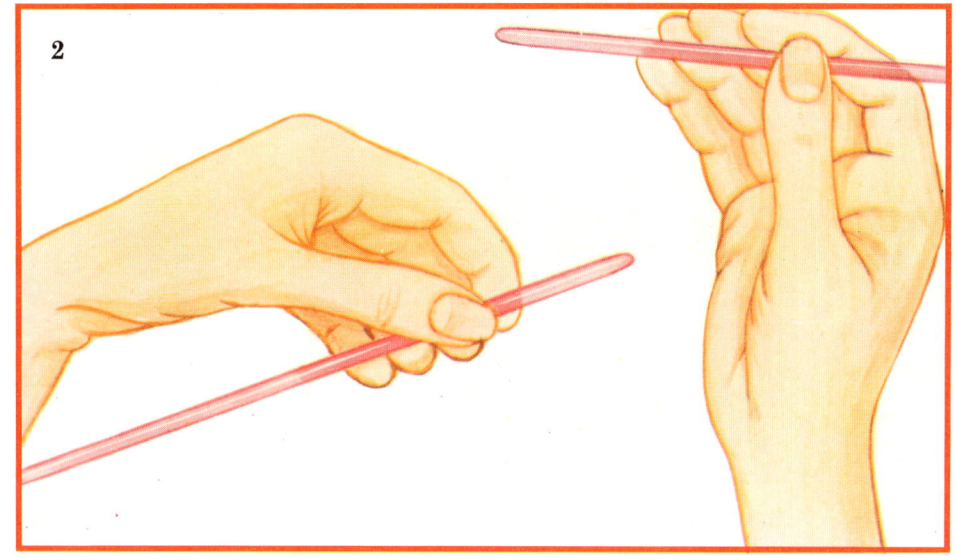

1. *The gas cylinder with valve and blowtorch attached.*
2. *The method used to hold the glass rods so that they may be rotated in the flame.*

for a glass rod to melt sufficiently for moulding. Use the tip of the paler blue flame for preheating the glass prior to melting it. It is imperative that the glass should be heated slowly, otherwise it will shatter and fragments of hot glass may fly out and cause burns. When the glass has been properly preheated and is ready to be melted, it will signal this by causing an orange flare in the blue flame. Move the rod to the hottest part of the flame for melting.

Several different techniques are used for moulding the glass. One rod can be attached to another by melting one end of each rod and pushing them together in the flame so that they melt into each other. Parts such as legs, wings, tails and ears are attached in this way.

To mould a leg, for example, the end of a rod is first attached to the body, then the length of leg is melted and the rod pulled out to the required shape.

Making balls of glass can be done by melting the middle of a rod and pushing both ends towards the middle so that a ball forms in the centre of the rod. A ball can be formed at the end of a rod by melting the tip of the rod, turning the rod all the time. The glass will retract into itself to form a ball.

A glass rod can be cut in half by heating and pulling apart. The thin strands of glass left on each separated end can be heated in the flame until they retract into the rest of the rod.

To harden rods that have been joined together or a piece that has been moulded, hold glass out of the flame for a few seconds, but never let the object you are working on cool down completely. If you put it down away from the flame for more than a few seconds, you may find that when you put the glass back in the flame it will crack or shatter. To keep the object on which you are working hot but not melting, always hold it in the paler blue part of the flame.

When you have finished your object, do not let it cool down quickly as this will also cause cracking. To prevent this happening, the glass should be cooled as slowly as possible in the coolest part of the flame, gradually withdrawing the glass from the flame.

Dachshund

Start with this simple piece which involves attaching and shaping the ears, four legs and the tail of the animal. Once you can make the dachshund successfully, and it will probably take several attempts, you will be able to use this basic shape for any four-legged animal.

Assemble tools and materials on asbestos mat or kitchen foil wrapped around a piece of wood.

Put on dark glasses. Turn on and light torch.

Hold one transparent rod in your left hand (this will be the body) and the other transparent rod in your right hand (this will form the legs).

Heat the tip of the left-hand rod over the flame until it starts to melt. Then heat the tip of the right-hand rod in the flame keeping the left-hand rod warm, but not melting, by holding it in the tip of the flame (fig.3).

When the tip of the right-hand rod has melted to a thick syrupey consistency, join it to the end of the left-hand rod slightly to one side.

Pull out and shape leg (fig.4) – if the glass is too soft the leg will be too thin. Try to get the glass hot enough to mould but not to run. Cut leg to the required length by heating at the required point and pulling off the rest of the rod. Press the tip of the leg on to the carbon block, or piece of brass, to form a foot with a flat base (fig.5).

Using the rest of the leg rod, attach the other back leg in the same way.

Heat the end of the transparent blue rod and attach to animal (fig.6). Pull the rod to stretch it out and hold away from the flame for a few seconds until it hardens – this will form the tail. The rest of the rod attached to the tail will serve as a handle while the animal is being modelled.

Turn the animal around and hold in the left hand by the tail (blue rod).

Dachshund

You will need:
A blowtorch.
Tweezers of various shapes and sizes.
A block of carbon about 10cm by 10cm by 2.5cm (4in by 4in by 1in) or a piece of brass 10cm by 10cm by 6mm (4in by 4in by ¼in).
A metal rack or glass jar for holding hot glass rods.
Box of matches.
A sheet of asbestos – but not blue asbestos.
Dark glasses.
Two yellow transparent glass rods 15cm (6in) long, 6mm (¼in) diameter.
One transparent blue glass rod, 6mm (¼in) diameter and long enough to serve as a handle (about 7.5cm (3in) long).
Miscellaneous pieces of coloured rod for eyes, nose, ears etc.

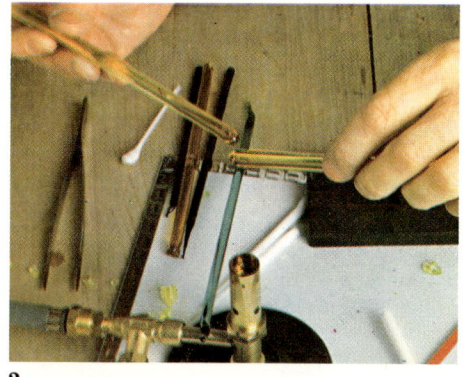
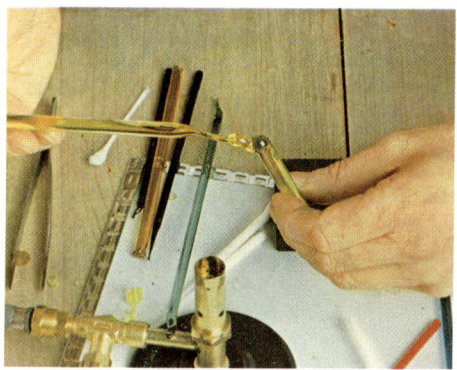

3 **4**

5

6

3. *Heating the two glass rods.*
4. *The rear leg is made by drawing the heated glass.*
5. *The carbon block is used to flatten the completed leg into a paw.*
6. *Attaching the tail to the body of the dachshund.*

Heat the body at a point about 5cm (2in) from the base of the tail and kink glass to form neck. Draw off the body glass to a taper to form the head and pull off the rest of the rod (fig.7).
Using the remainder of the rod that formed the back legs, attach

the front legs in the same way as the back legs, shaping them as shown in fig.8.

You have now made the main body of the dachshund. Next attach ears, eyes and nose.

Heat up the end of a red or brown rod and attach a small blob to the end of the nose.

Heat up an opaque white rod and attach two small dots for the eyes. Heat end of black rod and put two small dots in the middle

7

9

8

10

of the white dots. Hold in the flame until any strands of glass attached to the eyes disappear.

Heat about 6mm ($\frac{1}{4}$in) of the end of the brown glass rod and shape ears by flattening with tweezers (fig.9).

Heat the tip of flattened area and melt into one side of the head. Heat the attached ear in the flame and let it flop to the required shape. Heat ear with a small flame at the point where the ear should end and pull off excess.

Using the same brown rod, attach other ear to complete animal. Hold head of animal and heat attached tail at the point where it becomes a handle. Pull off handle (fig.10).

7. *Forming the head and neck.*
8. *The front legs are next.*
9. *Shaping the ears before attaching.*
10. *The completed animal.*

Swan

The basic shape of the swan can be modified to make other birds.
Place asbestos mat or kitchen foil wrapped around a piece of
wood on a flat surface, and lay out tools.
Put on dark glasses. Turn on and light torch.
To make the body and neck, take the white glass rod and hold at
both ends.
Heat a section 13mm (½in) long, about 5cm (2in) from left hand.
As the glass softens use both hands to push the ends of the rod
inwards to form a ball in the centre of the rod. This will be the
body of the swan. Press the ball against the carbon block.
Next, heat the rod along about 1.25cm (½in) directly to the right
of the ball. When soft pull gently and bend into an S-shaped
neck. You will find that when you pull out the soft glass it will
stretch and become thinner. Separate rod from end of neck.
Heat the end of the neck to form ball-shaped head.
Heat the end of an opaque black rod and attach two small specks
of black glass to the face for the eyes. Hold in the flames until
any strands of glass attached to the eyes disappear.
Heat the end of the yellow rod and the head of the swan and
attach yellow rod to head. Pull out yellow rod to form beak and
separate rest of yellow rod from beak.
Heat the end of the opaque white rod (the piece that was pulled
off from the head) and flatten about 6mm (¼in) of the end of the
rod with the tweezers. If the rest of the swan cools down while
forming the wing, pre-heat in tip of flame before attaching wing.
Melt flattened end of rod into one side of the swan and pull out
to form a wing. Separate rest of rod from the wing and form other
wing in the same way.
Heat the tail end and pull off the rod, leaving a pointed tail.
Gradually remove finished bird from the flame.

Swan
You will need : Tools as for the dachshund. Opaque white glass rod 13cm (5in) long, 6mm (¼in) diameter. Opaque black glass rod 7.5cm (3in) long, 3mm (⅛in) diameter. Yellow glass rod 7.5cm (3in) long, 3mm (⅛in) diameter.

*Below: The swans are described in
detail here. The same basic form
will make a variety of different
birds and animals.*

Leaded glass

SIZES OF LEAD CALMES		
The height (thickness) for both round and flat lead	Round lead—the leaf measurement	Flat lead—the leaf measurement
3mm ($\frac{1}{8}$″)	4.75mm ($\frac{3}{16}$″)	6.35mm ($\frac{1}{4}$″)
4.75mm ($\frac{3}{16}$″)	6.35mm ($\frac{1}{4}$″)	8mm ($\frac{5}{16}$″)
5.50mm ($\frac{7}{32}$″)	8mm ($\frac{5}{16}$″)	9.50mm ($\frac{3}{8}$″)
6.35mm ($\frac{1}{4}$″)	9.50mm ($\frac{3}{8}$″)	12.7mm ($\frac{1}{2}$″)
8mm ($\frac{5}{16}$″)	12.7mm ($\frac{1}{2}$″)	15.9mm ($\frac{5}{8}$″)
9.50mm ($\frac{3}{8}$″)	15.9mm ($\frac{5}{8}$″)	19mm ($\frac{3}{4}$″)
	19mm ($\frac{3}{4}$″)	22.2mm ($\frac{7}{8}$″)

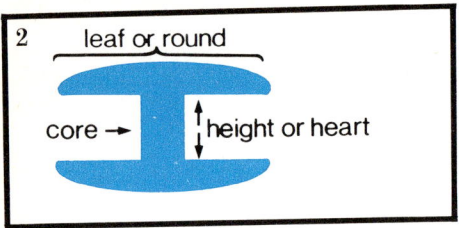

1. The various sizes of lead calme are shown in the chart.
2. The names of the different parts of a calme.

Introducing coloured glass and leading

In traditional glasswork, strips of leading are used to hold together the pieces of glass. This combination of glass and leading is very durable and has produced many glorious windows dating from medieval times. It is still the method used for making modern stained-glass windows.

Although leaded windows are usually made by professional glass workers the necessary techniques are not particularly difficult to learn.

Once you have cut and 'leaded up' a few pieces of glass you will be able to undertake such varied projects as glass window hangings, a terrarium for plants, or a Tiffany-style lamp. In this chapter the types, sizes and uses of leading are discussed, and examples are shown of the kinds of glass, including stained (or, more exactly, coloured) glass, which can be used in glass work.

Leading

Leading is either single channel or double channel ('H' section). Single channel is used for the edges of windows. A length of leading is called a calme and is produced in a variety of widths and thicknesses (fig.1). The calme core remains constant at about 1.5mm ($\frac{1}{16}$ in) thick. The different parts of a calme are shown in fig.2.

A calme is usually sold in 1.5m (5ft) lengths and two types are available: either flat or slightly rounded. The cross sections of both are symmetrical. The rounded version is stronger and better suited to normal leaded window work but is less flexible than the flat type.

To use the leading a calme is cut into lengths and the pieces of glass slotted into the channels. The calme is then soldered together at each intersection so that the separate panels of glass are surrounded by lead strip on all sides.

Antique glass

Traditional stained or coloured glass is normally called Antique glass and is sold in sheets. It is never perfectly flat or totally uniform in colour and is often grainy or streaky in texture. The colour is obtained from a combination of metal oxides which are added to the glass at the molten stage; an Antique glass might take the name of one of its chemicals, e.g. Selenium red. Strictly speaking, most glass known as 'stained' is, in fact, only coloured. (True stained glass is made by painting the glass with a mixture of silver nitrate and gamboge – a gum resin – which is subsequently fired to give a yellow stain.) Stained glass is the term, though,

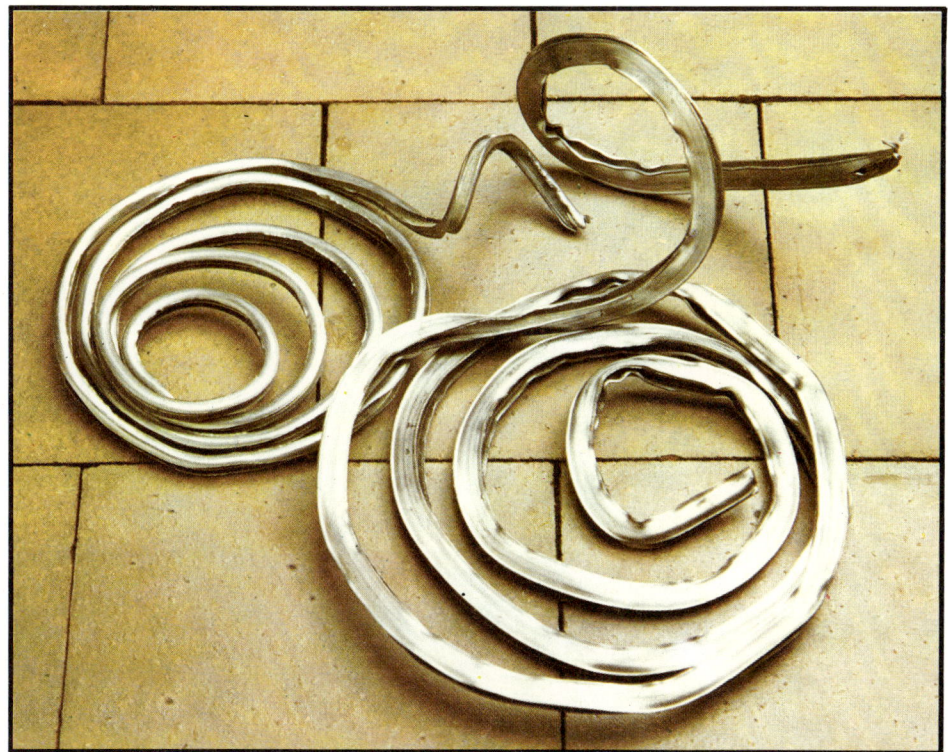

Left: Lead calme is sold in coils and requires straightening before use.

most popularly used to describe Antique glass.
The following are the main varieties of Antique glass:
Pot glass This is made in simple, single colours and comes in a regular thickness.
Flashed glass is made from a sheet of clear glass; one side is thickly coated with colour and the other side has only a thin skin of colour. The two coats need not be the same colour but can be a combination, e.g. red and white, red and light green etc. Hold flashed glass up to the light and look along the edge. The two layers of colour are usually distinguishable. This type of glass can be used for etching or the colour scratched away from the surface to make a design.

POT **SEEDY**

Above: An example of seedy glass (left) and cathedral glass (right).
Right: Various examples of Antique glass.

FLASHED **SLAB**

Seedy glass As its name implies the texture of the glass is like seeds or bubbles.

Streaky glass This type is distinguished by its irregular streaks which are hard to cut.

Reamy glass looks like streaky but is lighter in density of colour and comes in watery, translucent, pale shades. It is easy to cut.

Opalescent glass is a type of flashed glass, usually streaky, milky and translucent in colour. It is smooth in texture and is mainly used for Tiffany-style lampshades.

STREAKY

REAMY

PLATE CATHEDRAL OPALESCENT

Commercial glass

Commercial glass is made in a great variety of textures and finishes, including sandblasted, frosted and satin finishes. There are also various types of textured patterned glass. Commercially made glass is cheaper than Antique glass and comes in a number of types:

Plate glass is clear, white or smoky. It is smooth and is easy to cut.

Cathedral glass comes in a variety of textures and colour shades. It is cheap and useful to practise on before working with Antique

48

glass so don't worry if you break a few pieces in the early stages.
Slab glass or Dalles-de-Verre (flag-stone of glass). This is very
thick slabs of glass, 20mm ($\frac{3}{4}$in) to 31mm ($1\frac{1}{4}$in) thick. It is usually
set in concrete and used to make murals.

Mirror and leaded glass

Once you have started to use lead calme to hold together pieces
of glass you will find that the scope of your glasswork expands
enormously.

*Far left: A leaded mirror using
various kinds of Antique and
commercial glass.
Left: An inexpensive alternative
when practising, is to paint
ordinary glass with glass paints.*

When using lead for the first time it is a good idea to practise on a few odd bits of glass. In this way you will get the feel of the leading and you will avoid spoiling large sheets of glass which are sometimes expensive.

After practising on a little scrap glass you will be able to make the mirror shown here. The mirror is surrounded by four rectangles of Opalescent glass and four squares of textured commercial glass held together by lead calme soldered at the joins. You can chose any colours or types of glass or you can colour your own using glass paints as described on page 13 . Alternatively, paint the back of the textured glass with silver paint after it has been leaded, to provide a silvered effect.

Try your hand at decorative glass hangings like the ones illustrated. They look attractive hung in front of a window or other light source.

The mirror

This mirror is simple to make and you can use any glass which is at hand. Once you have leaded up one mirror and coloured glass project you can try a variety of other designs.

Place white cardboard on flat surface. Using the ruler and pencil draw a set of templates for the mirror to the sizes given in the materials list. Cut out the templates.

Lay the felt on a flat surface and put the Opalescent glass on top. Arrange the four rectangular templates on the glass leaving a space between each template. Draw round the templates with the felt-tip pen and remove the templates. If you feel at all unsure about your glass cutting ability you may prefer to draw one template at a time and cut that section of glass before moving on to the next.

Lubricate the glass cutter beforehand by wiping it with a piece of felt which has been soaked in light machine oil. Hold the cutter so that the handle rests between the first and second fingers and thumb, and the bottom of the hand remains clear of the glass. Using a ruler, score the surface of the glass along the line with the cutter. Draw the cutter towards you keeping the action smooth. Do not press too hard or back-track because the glass may break at a point where you do not intend it to.

The scoring should be completed in one operation, the object being to score the surface of the glass evenly so that the piece can be easily tapped apart. Once the score mark is made, turn the glass over and lightly tap it with the end of the glass cutter along the score line. Keep the glass flat on the table. It will start splitting but keep on tapping until the two pieces separate. Patience and a light hand are essential at this stage.

Small pieces of glass can sometimes be stubborn. If this happens put on the goggles and use the pliers or grozers to snap off the glass. Hold the glass between the pliers and firmly jerk down, away from your face. Do not worry if the glass is still a little ragged. The leading will cover minor deficiencies.

Wrap up any remaining glass for another occasion. Sweep up any splinters and fragments and wrap in newspaper before discarding. The four corner pieces are cut from commercial glass in the same way.

Untwist the lead, then stretch and straighten it. To do this place one end of the lead under the heel of your foot and grip the other end with the pliers. Pull the lead up and over your shoulder. If you do it in this way you will not hit yourself with the pliers should the lead slip.

Place the lead on a working surface and separate the leaves of the lead with an oyster knife or other similar knife. With a lead cutting knife cut the lead calme into these lengths:

Two lengths 17.5cm (7in).
Four lengths 21cm (8¼in).
Two lengths 28cm (11in).
Four lengths 4.5cm (1¾in).

Lay the calme flat on the hardboard and slot in the mirror, Opalescent glass and commercial glass as in fig.1. Trim the lead if necessary so that the glass fits snugly into the leaves. Use the lathekin to smooth down the edges of the lead.

Clean the ends of the lead joints with wire wool. This is important since solder will not adhere well to a dirty surface. Also clean the

Mirror continued.

Hardboard or smooth piece of wood at least 30cm by 25cm (12in by 10in). Thin white cardboard about 30cm by 25cm (12in by 10in).
Medium grade Sandpaper
Felt, thick cloth or newspaper for padding the glass.
Light machine oil and scrap of felt.
Lampblack or grate black (optional).
Linseed oil-based putty (optional).
Wire, about 0.8mm
thick, or strong jewelry chain (optional).

Left: Colourful glass hanging.
Above: A leaded mirror frame.

end of the soldering iron with wire wool.

Carefully hammer in nails around the leaded-glass to hold it in place.

Heat up the soldering iron. An old-fashioned iron can be heated over a bunsen burner or the flame of a gas cooker; an electric iron can be plugged into the household electricity supply. Always lay a hot soldering iron on an asbestos mat, never directly on to the unprotected working surface. Achieving and maintaining the right temperature of iron takes a little practice. Test for the proper temperature by melting a little solder in a metal lid and letting it cool. Rub the end of the iron on the solder and when it starts to flow you will know you have reached the right temperature. Turn off the electric iron occasionally to stop it overheating.

Once the iron is tinned – a smooth 'puddle' of tin should adhere evenly to the end – you are ready to start soldering.

Rub the joints of the individual pieces of leaded-glass with flux or a tallow candle to aid the flow of solder. Place the stick of solder close over the joint and touch with the soldering iron so that a small drop of solder falls on the joint. Spread smoothly over the joint with the tip of the iron. Be careful not to let the solder fall on the glass as the heat may crack it. Do this to all the joints.

When the soldering is completed on one side, remove the supporting nails, lift piece up and turn over. Solder the back in the same way.

Since the glass pieces will probably be of slightly different thicknesses they will rattle within the lead leaves, you can squeeze putty between glass and lead. Mix up a little lamp black with the putty and push it underneath the lead on both sides of the glass. Trim the putty close to the lead with a sharp knife.

Rub down the lead and the joints with sandpaper and polish with lampblack.

Thread a wire of chain round the outer groove in the lead and hang at eye level. Alternatively, prop mirror on a flat surface such as a dresser.

Glass hanging

The tulip hangings shown here were made from Antique pot glass and lead calme soldered at the joints. The stems are strong wire soldered to the base of the leaves. The hook at the top is thinner wire. Cut, lead and solder the hangings as described for the mirror. When making hangings you will probably need to cut circles and small, irregular shapes.

A radius cutter is the special tool needed for cutting circles or semi circles, but you can make a perfectly satisfacotry circle by

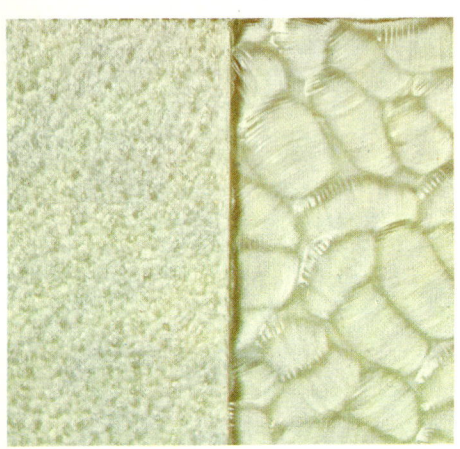

Top: Examples of commercial glass.
1. Dimensions for the leaded glass mirror.

using an ordinary glass cutter fastened to a length of string. The other end of the string is held down in the centre of the circle. The circles are much easier to cut if the cutter is drawn along in several long curves (fig.1). Three or four strokes of the cutter should be enough to cut an accurate circle. Hold the glass continuously while cutting each circle. Move bodily round the circle if this makes cutting any easier.

When cutting a point, cut the shape so that the point touches an edge of the glass (otherwise you will never manage to extricate the piece from its surrounding glass). Follow the cutting line as shown in fig.2.

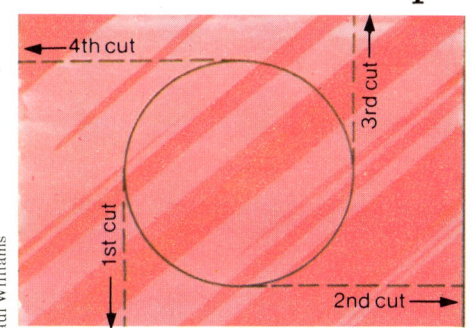

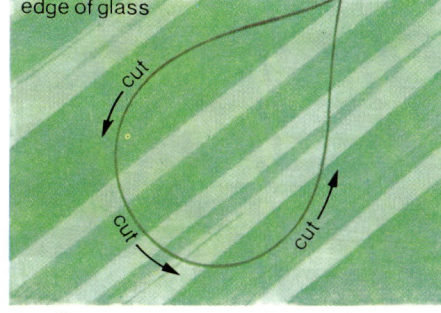

1. Cutting a circle from glass.   *2. Cutting a point from glass.*

Making a leaded terrarium

Once you have tried your hand at leading up a few pieces of glass and have perhaps made the mirror or a leaded window hanging you will be able to construct something larger.

A terrarium (or mini-greenhouse) is made with clear window glass and lead calme. Once planted with a variety of small plants, you will have a miniature garden which can be hung from a wall, either indoors or out, or stood on a table or shelf. The terrarium needs very little attention and is an ideal way of displaying your plants all the year round or even of growing a tiny herb garden.

Terrariums come in all shapes and sizes: square, cylindrical or conical. Some are completely glazed over with a removable lid, some are partially made of coloured glass and others are open at the sides. The terrarium shown here is open at the back for easy access and planting. It has five straight sides and a conical top made of five tapered pieces of glass. A back piece of glass retains the soil. Make a set of templates from cardboard as a pattern for the terrarium. To do this follow the measurements in fig.1 and fig.2, making sure that you have the angles correct for each piece. Draw each template on to the cardboard using pencil, ruler and protractor to measure the angles. Cut out the twelve templates. You

Above: Tulip hanging

53

Terrarium

You will need:

Tools as for the leaded mirror, see page 50 .

Window glass, 55cm by 40cm (22in by 16in) or other similar area of glass.

Lead calme: 3.65m (12ft) double-channel, round type, 8mm ($\frac{5}{16}$in) wide. 0.75m ($2\frac{1}{2}$ft) single-channel, round type, about 6mm ($\frac{1}{4}$in) wide. Both types of leading should be high enough to accommodate the thickness of glass.

Low-melting solder, 8mm ($\frac{5}{16}$in) thick.

Flux or a tallow candle.

Wire wool or wire brush.

Lasting nails or panel pins.

Small hammer.

Felt, thick cloth or newspaper.

Hardboard or smooth piece of wood at least 50cm by 50cm (20in by 20in).

Medium grade Sandpaper.

Masking tape.

Thin cardboard the size of the sheet of window glass.

Pencil, felt-tip pen, protractor. metal ruler and scissors.

Lampblack or grate black (optional).

Linseed oil-based putty (optional).

Epoxy adhesive (optional).

Strong wire or chain.

Right: The leaded terrarium.
1. Cutting plan for the terrarium.

SIDE PIECES

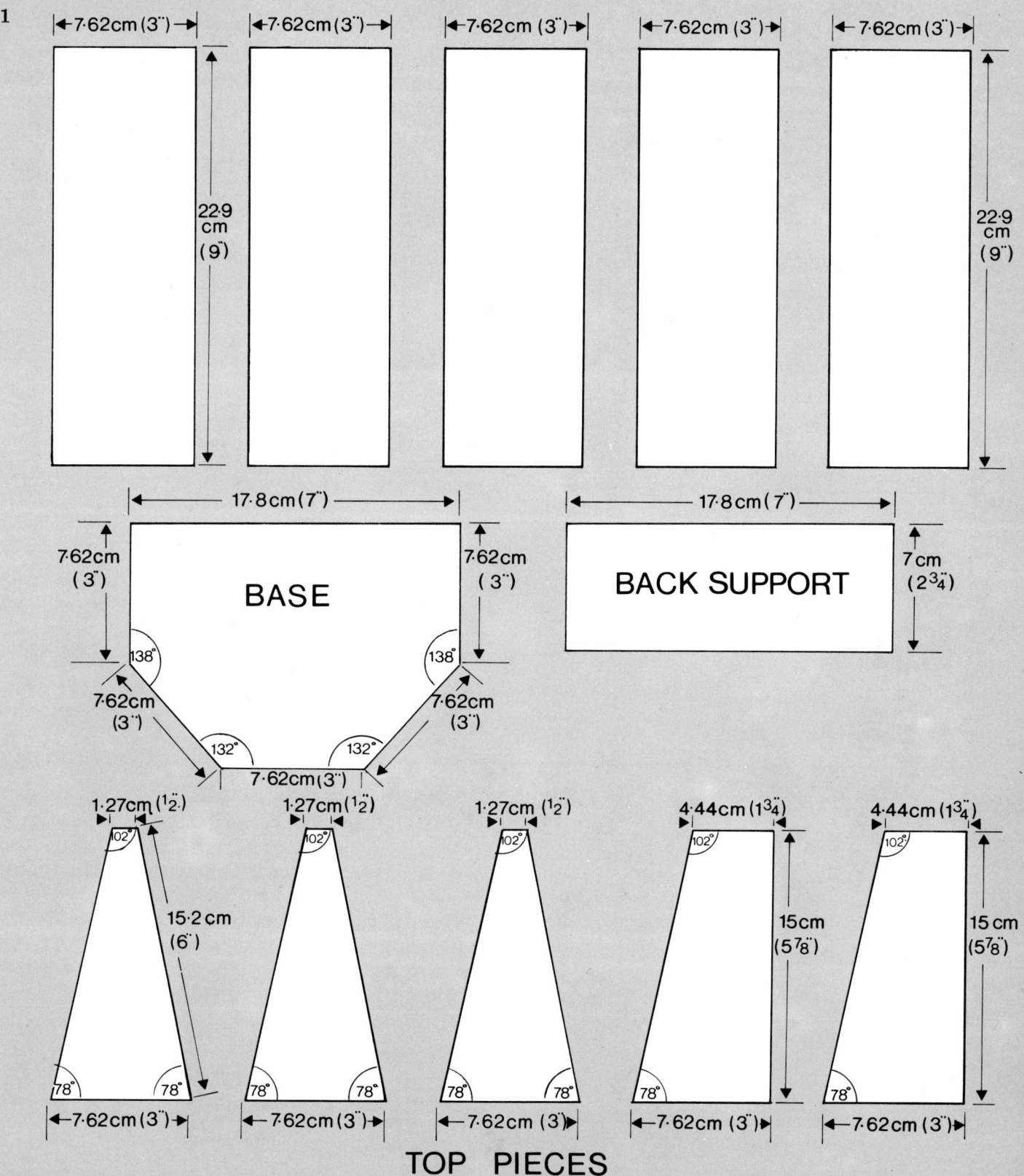

1

TOP PIECES

2. The glass and leading are joined in the sequence shown here. The joints marked 'x' are soldered.

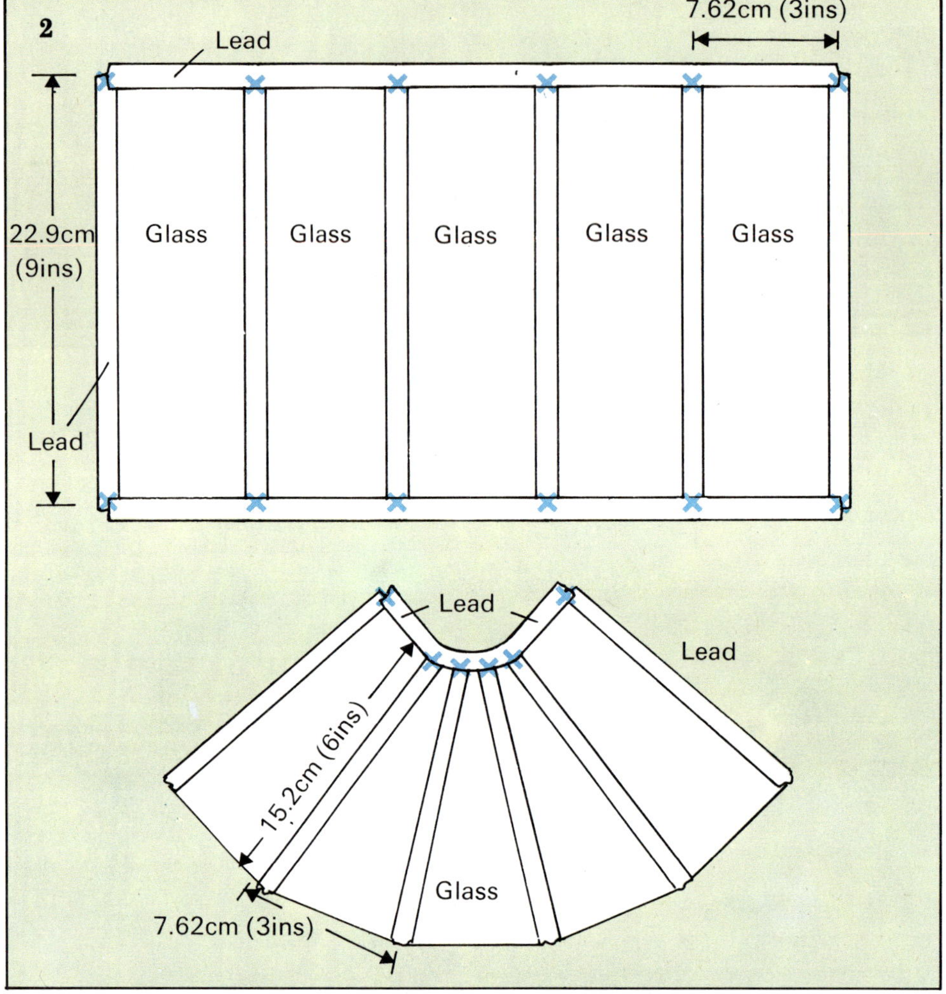

have five side pieces, five top pieces, a base and a back support. Lay the felt on a flat working surface and place the glass on top. Arrange the templates on the glass. They do not have to be arranged in any particular order so long as you get them all in. Leave enough space around the templates to allow for minor errors when cutting. Carefully draw round the templates with the felt-tip pen before removing.

Take the glass cutter in one hand and score the glass along the lines of the templates using a ruler to keep the lines straight. Turn the glass over and, with the end of the glass cutter, tap along the score line until the glass cracks. Follow the instructions on page 51 for cutting glass. Rub the corners with glasspaper until smooth. Untwist the lead, then stretch and straighten it using the method described on page 51. When the lead is quite straight lay it on

the working surface. With the cutting knife cut off sections of lead sufficient to hold the pieces of glass together. You will need the following lengths:
Double-channelled lead:
Six lengths 22.9cm (9in), for the sides.
Two lengths 38.1cm (15in), for the top and bottom of sides.
Six lengths 15.2cm (6in), for top pieces.
One length 17.8cm (7in); two lengths 6.5cm (2½in), for back support.
One length 12.6cm (5in) long, for 'horseshoe' shape round top pieces.
One length 3.2cm (1¼in) long, to join up two ends of 'horseshoe'.
Single-channelled lead:
One length 17.8cm (7in) and one length 38.1cm (15in) for the inside of the base.
One length 17.8cm (7in) for the back.
Open the leaves of the lead with an oyster knife or other strong, blunt knife. The handle of a pair of pliers can also be used for this process.
Slot the pieces of glass into the appropriate lead calmes and lay them flat on the hardboard as in fig.2. Do not slot in the base or back at this stage. You may find that you need to trim the lead at the corners of the glass with a cutting knife. Make sure that the pieces of lead lie neatly against each other at the joins. There should be no gaps between lead and glass although it does not matter if the glass rattles slightly so long as it is securely inside the leaves of the lead. Smooth the lead flat over the glass with a lathekin or other small piece of wood. Using the hammer place lasting nails or other suitable nails at intervals around the leaded glass to hold it firmly in position. You are now ready for soldering.
Before soldering clean the end of the soldering iron and all the lead joins with wire wool. Heat up the soldering iron and, following the method described on page 52 , solder all the joins of the lead surrounding the five side pieces of the terrarium. In fig.2 the soldering points are marked with an X.
Pull out the lasting nails, turn the glass over, replace the nails and solder on the other side. Next, solder the lead surrounding the top five sections of the terrarium. You will only need to solder at the top.
When all the sections are soldered lift the side pieces upright and very carefully bend them into position around the base glass. Do not force the lead; it will bend if you are firm but gentle. Wrap masking tape around the sides to hold them in position.
Similarly bend the top section and place in position above the

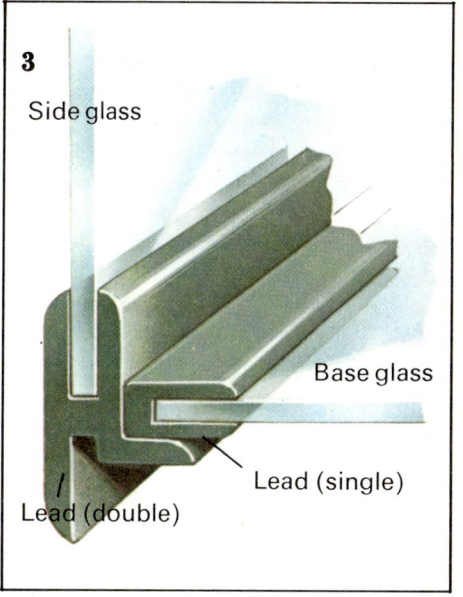

3. *Detail of the bottom edge of the terrarium.*

side pieces. The glass of the top sections will slot into the double-channelled lead of the side pieces. Solder the top sections to the side sections at the lead joins.

The short strip of lead 3.2cm (1¼in) long connects the back of the 'horseshoe' shape at the top of the terrarium. Stretch across the back just inside the outer edge and solder.

The glass base must be attached to the main structure of the terrarium.

Use the pliers to bend the inner leaf of the double-channelled lead at the bottom of the sides inwards and upwards to form a right angle (fig.3).

Bend the 38.1cm (15in) strip of single-channelled lead round the curved edge of the glass base, and slot in the glass. Take a 17.8cm (7in) strip of single-channelled lead and slot along the back edge of the base. Trim the lead at the corners if necessary. Solder the two joins together.

Place the leaded base inside the terrarium so it fits snugly on top of the right-angled lead (fig.3). Smooth under the outer edge of the double-channelled lead towards the centre of the terrarium for a neat finish.

For an extra strong finish turn the terrarium over and solder base to sides at intervals.

The back support is made from the remaining rectangle of glass. Fit 17.8cm (7in) of double-channelled lead along one long side of the glass and 17.8cm (7in) single-channelled lead for the other side. Slot the two short sides of the rectangle into the remaining leading.

Trim the four corners of the lead so they fit neatly against each other. Solder the corners together. Fit the back on to the terrarium, keeping the single-channelled lead uppermost.

Temporarily remove the glass base and solder the joins where the inner side and back leaves meet. Replace the base and solder the four points where the back leading meets the side leading. Any uneven edges should be finally smoothed over with the lathekin. The terrarium is perfectly usable as it is but water will run out of the bottom. If you prefer the terrarium to be water-proof, mix up a little lampblack with putty. Using an oyster knife press the putty between lead and glass around the base, the back and 7.5cm (3in) up the sides. Make sure that the putty fills the gaps for a tight seal. The lead of the base should also be firmly glued to the lead upon which it is resting. Use an epoxy adhesive for this.

The terrarium hook can be hung from a chain or a couple of twisted strands of strong wire soldered to the top. In the terrarium illustrated two lengths of solder were soldered to the top. Remember that the terrarium is quite heavy, especially when full of plants and soil, and will need a strong support.

Rub down the lead and clean up the joints with medium grade sandpaper, then polish with lampblack for a good shine.

Plant the terrarium as you would plant a pot but remember that terrarium plants will probably need less water than you expect.

Left: The back of the finished terrarium.

Tiffany-style lampshades

Louis Comfort Tiffany (1848-1933) was an American painter, craftsman and decorator. He produced a wide range of objets d'art, but he is remembered primarily for his iridescent Favrile glass and, more specifically, for his famous Tiffany lampshades. Tiffany-type lampshades have become very popular in recent years. They are often made with Opalescent or iridescent glass surrounded by lead calme soldered together to form a rigid frame. Mounted on an old lamp or hung from the ceiling, this type of lampshade gives a very turn-of-the-century look to any room.

Lampshade

You will need:
Tools as for the leaded mirror, see page 50 .
Yellow Opalescent glass, 60cm by 30cm (2 ft by 1 ft). If you find yellow glass difficult to obtain try another colour.
Amber Opalescent glass, 60cm by 30cm (2ft by 1ft).
Double-channelled lead calme, round type, 6. 6 mm ($\frac{1}{4}$in) wide and 3m (10ft) long.
Single-channelled lead calme, round type, 3mm ($\frac{1}{8}$in) wide and at least 85cm (2ft 9in) long.
Low-melting solder, 1.5mm ($\frac{1}{16}$in) thick.
Flux or a tallow candle.
Wire wool or wire brush.
Lasting nails or panel pins.
Small hammer.
Felt, thick cloth, or newspaper.
Hardboard or smooth piece of wood at least 60cm by 60cm (2ft by 2ft).
Medium grade Sandpaper.
Lampblack, or grate black (optional).
Thin cardboard 30cm by 7.5cm (12in by 3in).
Pencil, ruler, felt-tip pen, pair of compasses, metal ruler and scissors.
Lamp fitting and lamp base.

Right: The completed lampshade.
1. The lamp fitting.
2. The pattern for the glass.

The lampshade

The lampshade shown here is in the Tiffany style, simple to make from yellow and amber Opalescent glass, although you can choose any colours you wish. It has straight sides and probably looks best hung from the ceiling. Once you have made this shade you can progress to other, more elaborate versions.

Draw and cut out a template from the cardborad. Since each glass piece is the same size and shape as every other piece you will only need one template. Follow the measurements in fig.2 and start by drawing the 25.4cm (10in) central line first. The curved bottom edge is drawn with a pair of compasses set at 3.2cm (1$\frac{1}{4}$in) radius and the radius point of the compass on the central line at X. Then draw in the short top line and finally draw the side lines. Cut out the template.

Lay the felt or newspaper on a flat surface and place the yellow glass on top. Position the template on the glass at one corner and draw round it with the felt-tip pen. Repeat five times. You will have more glass than you need to allow for any breakages or difficulties in cutting.

Score the lines on the glass with a glass cutter, using a ruler to ensure straight lines. Follow the instructions for cutting glass on page 51 . Turn the glass over and tap along the score line with the other end of the glass cutter until the glass cracks open.

Repeat the process for the amber glass. When you have finished cutting the glass there will be six yellow pieces and six amber pieces, all the same size.

Put on a pair of goggles and with a pair of grozers or blunt pliers gently snap off small chips of glass at the corners of the narrow end of each piece of glass. The intention is to round the corners so the lead will bend more easily, and allow the panel to fold into a lampshade shape.

Stretch and straighten the lead as described on page 51 .

Using a lead cutting knife or cut-down palette knife cut twelve strips of double-channelled lead 23.5cm (9¼in) long. Open the leaves of the lead with an oyster knife or other strong knife. Hammer two nails into the hardboard about 20cm (8in) apart. Place a strip of lead against the nails.

Position a glass panel into the exposed channel in the lead and then, by adding glass and lead alternately, build up the body of the lampshade (fig.3). The lead calme should not be quite as long as the glass and should be placed so that a small amount of glass is

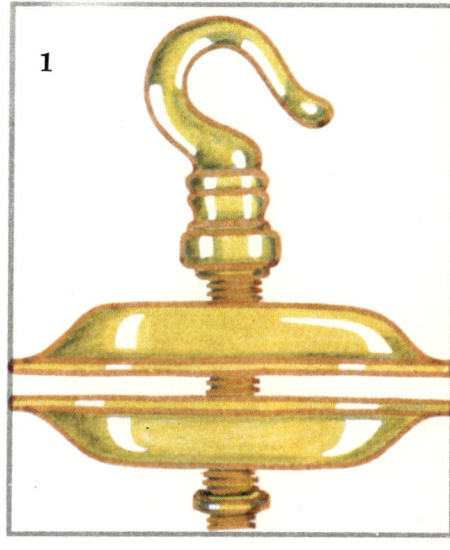

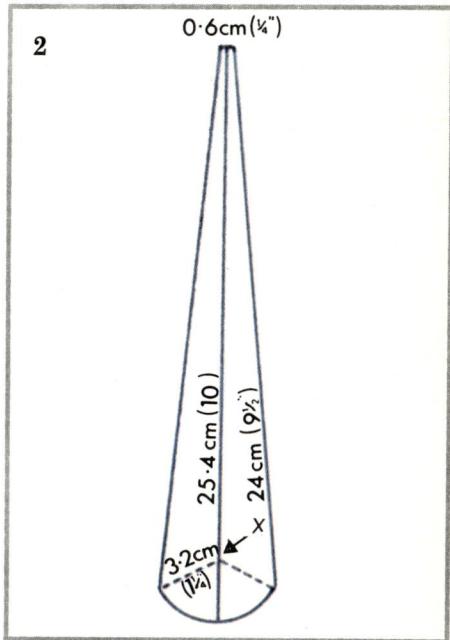

visible at either end. Remember to alternate the yellow and amber glass to create the design.

Tap each piece of glass into its channel as you position it and smooth down the lead on to the glass with a lathekin or small piece of wood. As each piece of glass is positioned, secure it with

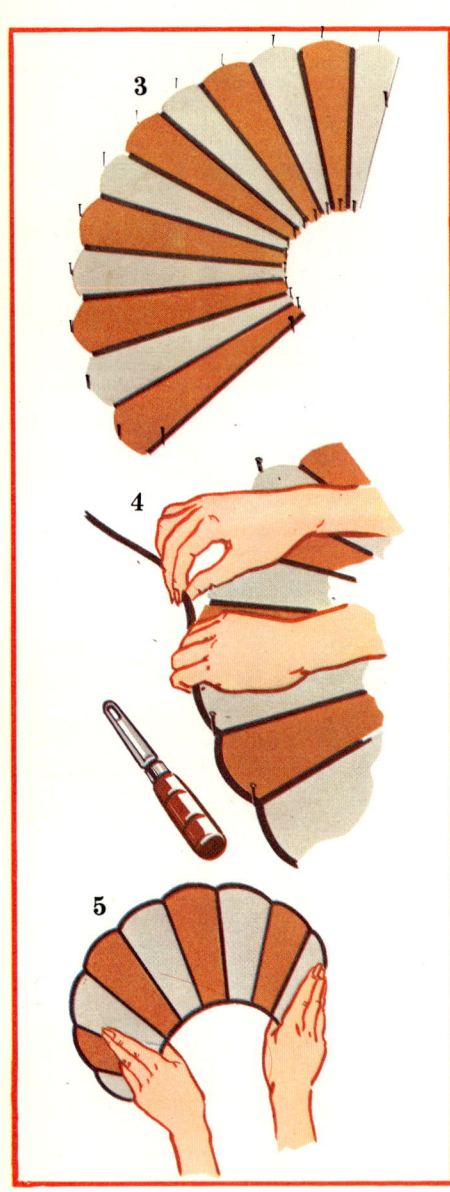

3. Strips of leading are alternated with the glass and held in place with nails.
4. The top and bottom leads are added checking each piece for close fit before soldering the joints.
5. After soldering, the lampshade is eased round and the final section soldered up.

a nail at top and bottom. The twelve panels, when assembled, form a fantail shape.

The next step is to add the top and bottom single-channelled lead. Starting at one end of the bottom border remove the nails one at a time and fit the single-channelled lead along the entire edge, panel by panel (fig.4). Make sure that the lead touches the ends of the double-channelled lead by pushing it up firmly into the joins between each panel. Replace the nails as you border each panel. When all the panels have been bordered cut the lead square with the outer edge of the twelfth panel. Repeat for the top border. All except the twelfth panel are laid out so they are housed on both sides with double-channelled lead. All twelve pieces are bordered at top and bottom edges with single-channelled lead, all pressed firmly together and held in position with nails. Only the outside edge of the twelfth panel is exposed; this will fit into the first strip of lead when the panels are bent round to make the lampshade shape.

Solder all the joins of the lead calme following the method described in making the leaded mirror on page 52 . Be sure to clean all joins with wire wool or wire brush before soldering. Make certain that solder does not run between glass and lead as this could cause difficulties when bending the panels. Be careful not to melt the strips of lead but, if you do, replace them immediately. After soldering the top side remove the nails, turn the glass over and solder on the reverse side.

Grip the top rim of the panels and raise them up while bending the two end panels round towards each other. Keep the bottom edge of the panels on the work surface to act as a brace. Keep an eye on the twelfth panel, which has no outside lead strip, to see that it does not slip out of place (fig.5).

Bend slowly and firmly to ensure that the glass does not pop out of the lead channels or crack.

After bending the panels of glass right round fit the remaining edge of glass on one side of the shade into the empty lead channel on the other side. Solder the top and bottom join on the inside and outside of this last joint.

Rub down the joins with medium grade sandpaper and polish with lampblack or grate black for a good shine.

Tiffany lamps were traditionally fitted with two 'vase caps', a nipple (threaded pipe) and a metal loop (fig.1). Buy these after making the lampshade. The lampshade is satisfactory, however, with an ordinary lamp fitting; it can also be hung from the ceiling.

After soldering the joint, shape the lampshade so that it is symmetrical and well rounded.

Mosaics

Introducing mosaics

History of mosaics

Mosaics is the craft of making designs and pictures by embedding innumerable small stones into a surface. It is so ancient a craft that no one really knows the meaning of the word; so modern a craft that even Picasso was happy to design for it.

The origins of mosaics go back to the very beginning of civilisation and early examples are found in many materials throughout the ancient world – lapis lazuli in Mesopotamia, ivory and glass in Egypt, colourful stones and pebbles in Greece. But it was the Romans, borrowing from the Greeks, who first developed the use of mosaic as decoration. Using the beautiful marble for which Italy is still famous, they made mosaic floors in their baths, fountains, homes, public buildings and squares. Even today any and all stones used in mosaic work are called tesse-rae, a word of Latin origin probably meaning four-sided.

Above: Detail of flooring mosaic from an Italian basilica.

Glass is nowadays the favourite material for making mosaics. In about the third century AD the Italian Christians discovered the wonderful colours and effects of light refraction that glass offers when cut into squares, called smalti.

The early Christians discovered how to produce gold smalti so that artists might show the supernatural aura surrounding the Deity. Thus arrived that lustrous and magical effect produced by gold which distinguishes Christian mosaics of the fifth century onwards from all that went before.

Gradually the use of gold smalti spread until, in sixth-century Ravenna, it became the entire background. The play of colour and light, the mixture of semi-precious stones and glass, the sheer life that these mosaics have when seen shimmering on the walls of a darkened church is unparalleled anywhere in the world.

Gold smalti were made in Ravenna, as they are made today, by fusing a thin layer of gold leaf between two pieces of glass, but the methods of applying them have changed. Originally a plaster of slaked lime and sand was applied to a wall and the artist, called the 'imaginary' in old documents, drew his previously prepared

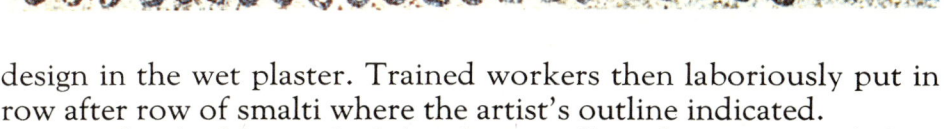

design in the wet plaster. Trained workers then laboriously put in row after row of smalti where the artist's outline indicated.

Present-day building schedules do not allow for artists and their assistants to sit around on scaffolding for several years, so craftsmen must lay out the whole mosaic on sections of paper and fix them into the wall in large blocks as quickly as possible.

Obviously it is beyond the scope of the beginner to try to reproduce in tesserae any of the mosaics illustrated here, but it can be done with remarkable ease using paper. This makes a handsome decoration as well as giving a genuine sense of the mosaic technique – the pleasure of it and the problems that the craftsman must solve, such as the use of colour, shaping of squares to fit the design and, very important, the sense of correct spacing. Practice in designing and making paper mosaics will be invaluable when it comes to producing the real thing.

Above left: A section of the vaulted ceiling from the sixth century tomb of Galla Placidia in Ravenna.
Above right: A detail of the vaulted ceiling at Ravenna.

Paper mosaic

Copying a Ravenna mosaic

First study the detail of the ceiling from the tomb of Galla Placidia, then look at the line drawing and photograph on page 65 .

Basically the design is a formal multi-petal flower surrounded by six circles and two alternating leaf motifs. It is really quite simple and this is the first thing about mosaic that beginners should understand: the basic design, whatever the project, needs to be strong and simple. The quality of the finished work will come from the colour and texture.

Right: The completed paper mosaic.
Far right: The pattern for the mosaic. This may be enlarged using a pair of compasses and a ruler. The central circle measures 3.8cm. (1½in) in diameter; it is quite a simple matter to work out the other dimensions from this area.

Cut the paper into 12mm (½in) strips and then into squares. Cut freehand. Keep each colour in a separate saucer or lid so that you can easily find the right shades when you are working.

To find the centre of the grey cardboard, draw diagonal lines from the corners. The centre will be the point where they cross. Now draw lines in the shape of a cross from left to right and top to bottom as in the diagram (fig. 1). This will give you the basic linear structure of the mosaic design and the eight gold leaves.

Take nine gold squares and place them in the centre circle. The four side pieces will need to be shaped to fit the circle (figs. 2). When you have positioned these lightly glue the back of each one and press it into place. Do not attempt to pre-glue several at a time, they just curl up and will be wasted.

When the gold circle is completed, take a clean piece of paper, put it over the area of mosaic and really rub it down; this ensures that all the edges are stuck.

To lay the petals, note first that they are shaded, a mid-blue next to the gold, then pale blue changing to white, and not all of them exactly alike. This is the art of mosaic which is to produce subtle variety in very simple ways. A certain primitive quality made by the irregularities is part of the charm of mosaic.

Since each petal is 7.2cm (3in) it would seem you should use six rows of tesserae, but this is not so. You need only five, as you must allow spaces between the stones for cement. To get this effect when you are using paper, simply leave the grey of your cardboard to show through to represent cement.

Use full-size squares down the middle of your petal and cut wedge-shaped ones to fill in the sides. A careful look at the reproduction will show you the best way of doing this. When you have gained experience you will be able to stick as you go, but to begin with arrange each petal before gluing individual squares.

When you have completed all nine petals, put a heavy weight on your cardboard and let it dry flat.

Start by filling in the navy blue background as you did for the petals, pre-cutting your wedges and pressing it as you go.

Then tackle the pale blue circle. When you have what seems a good, even spacing all the way round, glue the squares into place. Staggering the spacing is one of the constant problems in mosaic and it arises when you come to the double blue circle. If you place the squares accurately in line with each other, as in fig.3a you get lines running through both ways and also more cement showing But if you stagger the joins, as in fig.3b, you get a better visual arrangement.

When laying the double circle you will see that it is impossible to

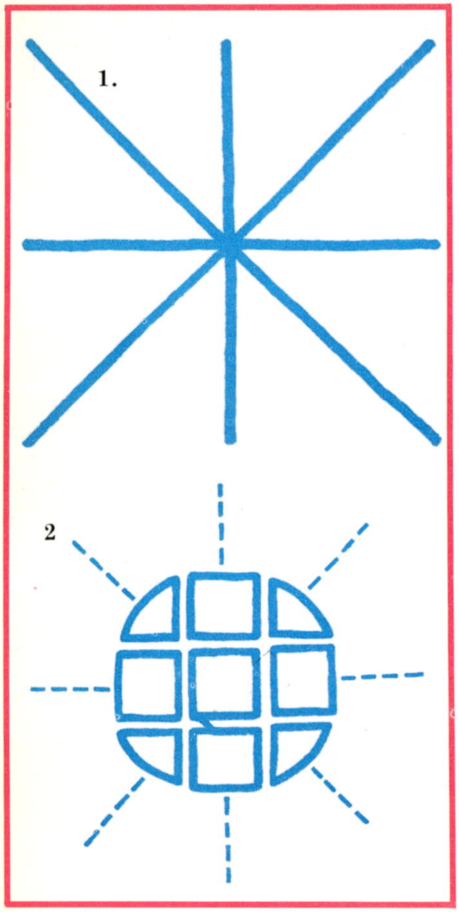

1. The centre of the sheet of card may be found by constructing diagonals from the corners. A vertical line is dropped through the centre and a horizontal line through the same point.
2. The central circle is made on the construction described above.

68

stagger the squares throughout since more squares are needed to complete the second circle. In this case it is probably best to start by staggering the joins of the first circle in relation to the joins of the pale blue circle and to let the second dark blue circle look after itself.

Next lay the single white circle and the double gold one. Notice how uneven the outer edge of the gold circle is, how it moves in and out of the navy blue subtly suggesting that it is a rosette.

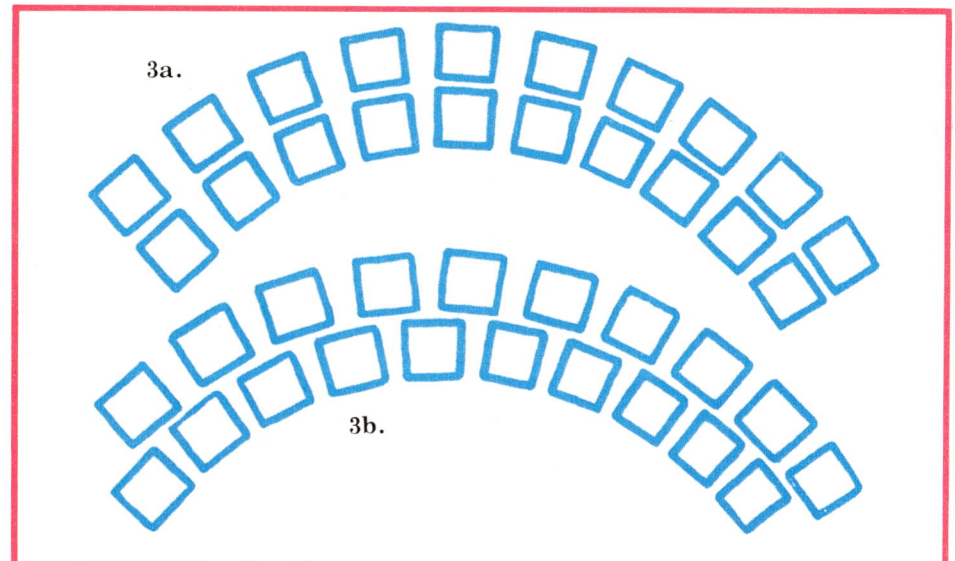

3a.

3b.

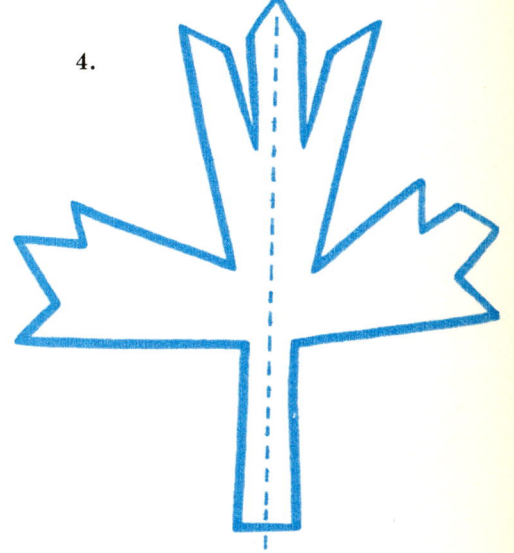

4.

Copy this effect using gold and, subsequently, navy squares and then add the final circle of gold.

Take a large sheet of clean paper, rub it right over the surface.

Again put the whole thing under weights to dry.

You are now ready to draw the surrounding leaf motifs. The larger ones will be about 15cm (6in) from base to tip. In the original mosaic each leaf varies slightly and by drawing each one freehand around the existing lines, as in fig.4, you can get the same effect. This applies also to the little blue leaf tips which are about 7.2cm (3in) in length and placed centrally between the gold leaves. When they have been sketched in, glue the gold leaves and then the blue ones, taking care to shade the two blue colours and to add a gold edge on the tip as illustrated. Press to dry.

To fill in the background in dark blue, note how the squares start by following the circle pattern and then gradually. almost imperceptibly, ease out to run in straight lines.

If the cardboard you are using is larger than you wish to fill, after the mosaic is completely dry, shear off the edges.

3a. The wrong way to lay the squares for the circles. This method would leave too much space between the squares.
3b. This method creates a much better visual effect.
4. The outline of the leaf motif.

Interior mosaic

Glass cullet mosaics

After making a paper mosaic you may like to try the technique used for making the fish panel illustrated. In this method glass cullet (broken glass) is stuck onto a plain sheet of glass in a free-hand design and ordinary tile grout is used to fill in the gaps between the cullet. The grout gives an opaque line to the design. The light will shine through the glass but not through the grout. An added advantage is that the grout will cover up all the sharp edges of the glass, even if the pieces of cullet are of marginally different thicknesses.

A bag of small pieces of coloured cullet can usually be bought by weight as off-cuts from most glass merchants. You will be lucky if you can get hold of red glass since this is more expensive than other colours. Alternatively, you could buy small sheets of stained glass from a stained glass supplier and cut them to shape yourself. Glass mosaic tesserae can be bought from most craft shops and these will do at a pinch.

One way of breaking glass into small pieces is to wrap it in several sheets of newspaper and gently tap with a hammer to create random shapes. Unwrap the newspaper carefully, pick out the pieces required while wearing canvas gloves, and carefully wrap the newspaper round the remaining glass fragments before discarding safely. Do not sweep your hand against glass fragments. This method of breaking glass is particularly suitable for any 'found' glass which you wish to use as cullet for a design. Look in the kitchen and the medicine cupboard for plain, green and blue bottles. The bottoms of these bottles will give flat pieces of glass and you can use the sides for curved shapes. Bicycle reflectors and brake lights give red glass. Look around you and see what you can find.

Lay down newspaper and rub the edges of the sheet of window glass with moistened silicon carbide paper to remove any sharp, jagged points. The silicon carbide paper should be wrapped around a sanding block for this operation, never simply hold in the palm of the hand. Failure to observe this rule could result in a nasty cut.

Sort through your cullet, selecting different shapes, sizes and colours. Draw the basic outlines of the fish on a piece of paper. Mark the various colours you have used. Firmly tape the design to the underside of the glass sheet.

Wipe the glass with white spirit or paint thinner to remove grease. Lightly rub the edges of each piece of cullet with silicon carbide paper on the sanding block. This is a fiddly job but a precaution against cuts and scratches.

Put a drop of adhesive on to each piece of cullet and, following the design, hold in position until stuck. The adhesive will show when it is hard so bear this in mind when applying it. Use the very small pieces for filling in odd gaps. Work quickly as epoxy-type adhesive hardens in a minute or two.

When all the cullet is stuck fast, fill in the spaces between with tile grout coloured brown or grey with powder colours. Follow manufacturers' instructions for mixing the grout.

The mosaic will look best if placed in front of a window or other source of light.

Above: The completed glass cullet fish mosaic.

Beginning to lay mosaics

Mosaic tabletop

A mosaic tabletop is not a difficult project for a beginner. In a big, bold table design the tesserae do not necessarily need cutting You simply lay them down in a pattern.

Another advantage of starting mosaic with a large item such as a

Below: This attractive mosaic tabletop uses a Greek key motif as the basis for its design. The squares require no cutting and the result has a bold quality.

table is that suppliers may not sell less than 30cm sq (12 sq in) of tesserae in any given colour, so to begin you may automatically become the owner of a considerable quantity.

Making a mosaic tabletop is at some stages a pretty messy business because it involves mixing cement. It is therefore a great asset to have a work area such as a junk room, garage or attic where you do not have to be too careful of your surroundings and where you can leave the work undisturbed to dry for several days.

There are many kinds of stones, or tesserae, that can be used in mosaic – marble, glazed and unglazed ceramic tiles and smooth pebbles, to name just a few – but the classic mosaic material is glass.

Vitreous glass squares can be bought in a standard size of 2cm ($\frac{3}{4}$in) from any mosaic dealer. The front of each square is perfectly flat and the back is bevelled as illustrated in fig.1. The bevelled side has a pattern or grid of lightly incised lines. Both features are designed for better grip and adhesion when the squares are applied to a surface.

The price of glass mosaic varies greatly according to the colour range, gold – as you might imagine – being the most expensive. You can work the design illustrated or you can plot your own design on graph paper as long as you stick to designs that involve the use of squares (fig.2).

Cross stitch embroidery and canvas-work patterns are a good source of ideas since each little square can represent one tessera. Another source of inspiration could be a modern geometric painting such as one by the Dutch painter, Piet Mondrian (1872-1944). Remember that the designs must be confined to those with straight lines and right angles which do not involve cutting or shaping the square tesserae.

Preparation

Put different colours of tesserae into separate jars so that you can easily find the colour you want when you are ready to begin.

Decide on a proper working area, preferably one in which you can leave the mosaic for a time (the messy stages come later). Place the blockboard on a work table and tape the sheet of paper securely to it.

Divide the working sheet into graph-like squares, each square representing one piece of mosaic (fig.2). Since the size of your table (and paper) is 48cm by 96cm (18in by 36in) and each tessera is 2cm ($\frac{3}{8}$in), it looks at first glance as though there should be 48 squares in the length and 24 in the width, but this is not so. You have to allow for cement joins between each square.

Mosaic tabletop
The materials below are given for a tabletop 48cm by 96cm (18in by 36in).

You will need:
Sheet of paper 48cm by 96cm (18in by 36in).
Marine plywood 48cm by 96cm (18in by 36in) and 13mm ($\frac{1}{2}$in) thick.
Polyvinyl acetate (PVA) glue –the waterproof setting variety – 0.28 litre ($\frac{1}{2}$ pint).
Vitreous glass mosaic in the colours you require, 0.5sqm (5sqft).
Fine-grade grey cement, two by 3kg (7lb) bags.
Large plastic container for mixing cement.
Trowel.
Cement comb (optional).
Old rags, and rubber gloves.
Jars for storing tesserae.
Thick, blunt pencil. Ruler.
Graph paper.
Nylon scouring pad.
Adhesive tape. Paper adhesive.
Silicone wax or furniture polish.
Gloss paint.
Metal table frame, or hardwood beading and wooden legs for the frame.

So divide your paper into 46 squares in length and into 23 squares across. In this way each square will be only a fraction larger than 19mm($\frac{3}{4}$in) and the difference is made by using a blunt pencil which gives a thicker line round each square. This may sound imprecise, but you will see how it works out as you progress.

When the grid is completed, fill in the actual shape of the pattern lightly with pencil. Use the colours in the mosaic if you wish. Now you are ready to begin laying the tesserae.

Laying tesserae

Tesserae are not laid directly into cement. Instead, each square is glued with paper adhesive face down on to paper and the whole design is imbedded into the cement later on. Although this is a much easier way of working it means that for the time being you will be working in reverse. The mosaic will be stuck face down, leaving the bevelled side facing you. (As this design does not have an 'up and down' or 'right and left' side, you will not have to worry about actually thinking in reverse.)

Start at the top left hand corner of the paper. Pick up the mosaic stones one at a time and give each a dab of glue on the flat, i.e. right, side. Then put each stone firmly into place, face down, leaving the thickness of black line between each tessera (fig.3). Do not use too much glue or the paper may buckle. Worse still, the tesserae may slide around and fail to keep their place in the design. Work about 30sq cm (1sq ft) in this way and then weight the mosaic down with heavy books to dry in the same way as you did for the paper mosaic (page 68).

Before you lay each piece of mosaic, examine it closely. Being mass-produced, some tesserae are imperfect and whereas a certain irregularity is part of the charm of glass mosaic, pieces that are badly misshapen or have broken corners should be rejected. (They can come in useful later when you start to cut mosaic.)

When the entire mosaic has been laid, leave it under weights for a few hours until you are absolutely sure it is dry.

Cementing

If until now you have been working in a room with a carpet or household furniture near or under you, the moment has come to move – to the garage if necessary. Failing any such place, spread a sheet of polythene to protect the floor where you are working and put several layers of newspaper on the table. No matter where you work you will need a flat surface to hold the board and you will need to leave it there for several days after it is cemented.

Remove or cut the tape binding the paper to the board and care-

1. The faces of tesserae are smooth, the edges are bevelled and the back carries in incised grid.
2. Use graph paper for your design and enlarge to the required size.

fully slip the board from underneath the tesserae-covered paper. Prepare the board by priming each side with a mixture of one part water-soluble glue (remember it must be the kind that sets water-proof) and three parts water. You will eventually need as much as 1.2 litre (2 pint), but this can be mixed in several batches if you prefer. Allow one side to dry for two hours before priming the other. When you have finished be sure to wash your brush out well. Once it has dried the glue is no longer water-soluble. For priming do not use a brush which has a trace of oil or turpentine on it as this may wreck the cement adhesion.

If the priming brings up the grain of the board, and makes it rough to touch, so much the better because it will help to provide better adhesion for your cement mixture.

Up to 0.9kg (2lb) of cement is needed for every 30sq cm (1sq ft). For the table put about 2.7kg (6lb) into a mixing container and make a hole in the middle as if you were making pastry.

Gradually pour in some of the same glue mixture used for priming the board. Stir well until you get a fluffy paste, rather like whipped cream, which just about keeps its shape. It is impossible to say how much liquid you will need but, broadly speaking, 0.5 litre (1 pint) should be enough. Take great care not to add too much glue, however. To soften the mixture, work it well rather than adding more liquid.

When you have the right consistency – and this will take some hard work – spread the mixture evenly with a trowel over the backs of the tesserae. The joins between the stones will fill up as you spread the first layer. Continue until the whole mosaic is covered with an even layer of cement about 3mm ($\frac{1}{8}$in) thick. The outlines of the tesserae will be barely discernible.

Then, immediately as you have no time to lose, mix another batch of cement with glue mixture but this time only 1.4kg (3lb) – half as much as before – and spread it on the board in a thin, even coat. If you use a cement comb for spreading the cement you will find it easier to get an even distribution.

You must now unite the two cemented surfaces by putting the board down over the sheet of mosaic. If possible, get someone to help you lower the board on to the tesserae as it is difficult to manage alone and once put down there is little possibility for adjustment.

When it is in place, cover the top of the board with weights (fig.4) and leave it for a week. If you are using an old work table you might drive a couple of nails half-way in on each side of the board (not through it) to keep the mosaic from being jostled. Be sure to check the outside edge of the mosaic and push back in place any over-

3

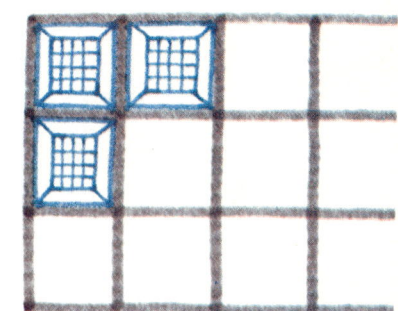

4

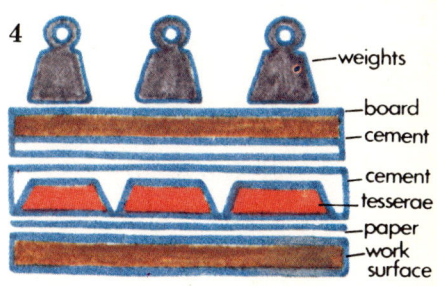

weights
board
cement
cement
tesserae
paper
work
surface

3. Each tesserae is glued face down on the paper leaving a space the width of the pencil line.
4. After applying the cement to the backs of the tesserae and the board, the work must be left under weights to set.

flowing cement.

If the work is to be left in a garage or other outbuilding, make sure there is no chance of frost.

Throw left-over cement into a waste bin, not down the drain, and wash out the mixing bowl and trowel thoroughly. Keep any diluted glue because it will be needed at the end of the week. Unmixed cement can also be kept if the bag is carefully closed and kept away from moisture.

Cleaning the surface

The final stage consists of taking off the weights and turning the board right side up so that the surface can be cleaned and grouted. Facing you will be a rather stained piece of paper with the dim outline of the underlying tesserae.

Right: The completed mosaic. The pattern for the design may be made by following the diagram.

Resist the temptation to pull the paper off. Get a rag and a bowl of hot water and soak the paper well, going over and over it until the hot water penetrates to the gum beneath and you feel it ready to move. At this stage your paper should come away in two or three big sections – if not, then go on wetting it patiently.

When it is finally revealed, the design will still be in need of a good deal of cleaning to get rid of the gum on the surface and any remaining bits of paper which have stuck in the joins. Possibly some cement will have moved forward to the front of the design. Scrub vigorously with a nylon scouring pad and hot water. Do not use a metallic cleansing pad as tiny particles will get into the cement and rust.

There will be many small gaps between the squares and these must now be filled. Use the same diluted glue and cement mixture as

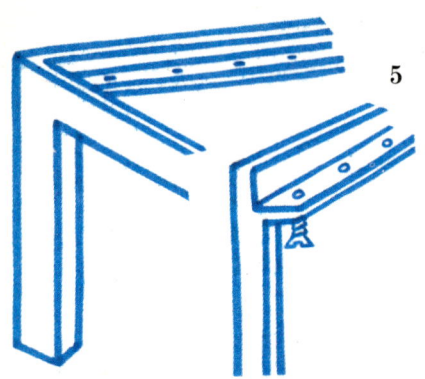

5. The coffee table is completed by fixing the mosaic to a frame. This can either be made at home or purchased ready made. In this case it is a simple matter to screw the frame to the board from underneath.

before, only this time rub it into the front of the mosaic so that it fills in any remaining gaps in the joins.

This is a rather discouraging moment. No sooner is the surface clean than you must make it dirty again. You can use your fingers to rub the cement into the joins or you can use a large screwdriver or other similarly shaped tool. When all the joins appear to be filled take a handful of absolutely dry cement and sprinkle it over the surface. Make a firm pad out of an old rag and rub it vigorously all over the mosaic. The dry cement will be pushed partly into the joins and partly over the edge of the board. The harder and faster you rub, the tighter and better grouted the joins will be.

Now sweep up all loose particles of cement and leave the mosaic overnight to set. It will look rather grey and dusty but no actual lumps of cement should be stuck to the surface.

Wash the surface the next day with detergent liquid and hot water, drying it as you go.

If it still looks grey (the grain of some mosaic has a stronger tendency than others to pick up cement dust) dip some absorbent cotton in pickling strength vinegar (acetic acid), available from pharmacies, and rub it all over the surface. The acid will neutralize the alkali of the cement and the grey will disappear.

When thoroughly dry, wax with a good, colourless silicone wax or furniture polish. This will bring out the colour and also help to make the joins more resistant to spilt liquids and general dirt. Finally, paint the underside of the board with a coat of gloss paint. This will prevent the wood from warping and counteract any slight warp that may have developed during the drying process because of inadequate weighting.

There are two simple ways to turn your slab of mosaic into a coffee table. The simplest is to buy a metal table frame, constructed for the purpose, and screw the board into the angle irons (they have holes already drilled in the iron for this) (fig.5). You must grout in the little gaps which will inevitably exist between your mosaic and the metal frame. This can be done during the final grouting, described above, to save additional cleaning of the surface.

Alternatively, you can frame the mosaic with strips of hardwood beading 2.5cm by 6mm (1in by ¼in) glued to the sides of the board. The wood should have two coats of polyurethane varnish before you attach it so that it will not change colour or be affected by any spot grouting which may be necessary round the edges. The frame should be masked before you grout any gaps. To complete the table, buy a set of wooden legs and attach these by screwing into the board underneath.

Cutting
and designing

While many attractive, and sometimes quite spectacular, results can be achieved with standard 2cm ($\frac{3}{4}$in) square vitreous glass tesserae, designs must be limited to geometric and abstract patterns based on squares. Once you have learned to cut square tesserae into other shapes, however, the design range is extended enormously. This chapter shows how to cut pieces to any shape required and how to design your own mosaics.

Cutting

In the past, mosaic was always cut with special hammers and, more recently, with little guillotines which are still used in Italy. But by far the easiest way to tackle cutting is with the modern mosaic nippers which are available at most mosaic stockists. These nippers have special tungsten-tipped blades and, after a few hours practice,

Left: This coffee table was made using a design that requires the cutting of the tesserae. As the photograph indicates, the scope is much wider as it is possible to use curved as well as straight edged designs.

you should be able to cut a few basic shapes.

Practise first on any rejects – pieces from earlier projects which were unusable because of broken corners or distorted shape. Remember to wear goggles to protect your eyes.

Rectangles Grasping both sides of a mosaic square firmly between thumb and first finger of your left hand (if you are right handed), insert the nipper blades no more than 6mm ($\frac{1}{4}$in) along the mosaic square and press the handles firmly together.

There should be a resounding click as the mosaic splits neatly into two halves. If you let go, or do not hold firmly enough with your left hand, the pieces will fly all over the room. If you find you have to press with enormous force with the right hand it probably means that you have the nipper blades too far into the mosaic when cutting. Glass breaks essentially by vibration: all it needs is a sharp shock at one end to start the break on its way – for the rest of the way it travels by its own momentum.

Do not be discouraged by early failures; all you need is practice, not physical strength. Do not practise for too long the first time – an hour is plenty. By the end of this time you will have a fair stock of little rectangles, and inevitably, some badly-cut, useless glass. Try to turn some of the failures into little squares as they will be very useful.

Triangles It is a little more difficult to make triangles as the mosaic piece must be held at an angle to the nippers. It is almost impossible to get two equal-sized triangles out of one square, so be prepared to accept a cut that gives one triangle that is distinctly larger than the other (fig. 1) – both shapes will be useful.

Curved shapes Having mastered the cutting of angular pieces, proceed to curved shapes. By a process of 'nibbling' with the

Below: From left to right, using the special cutters to cut rectangles, triangles and curves.

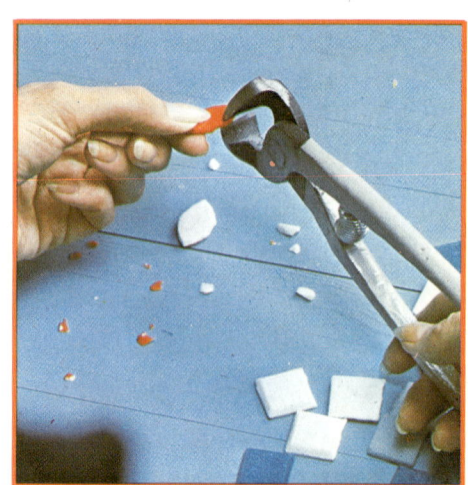

nippers – making a series of small cuts – it is possible to cut the basic 19mm ($\frac{3}{4}$in) squares into: a leaf shape (fig.2a); or a half leaf (fig.2b), enabling you to make a two-tone leaf; and various curved 'triangles' (figs.2c and d).

In no time at all, a whole vocabulary of shapes can be made and used to build a simple design.

Designing

When you have amassed a variety of shapes – rectangles, triangles, small squares and curved shapes (fig.3a) – move them around to see how they can be combined, adding more as required (fig.3b). Every so often you will be left with a space into which nothing seems to fit. Try then to cut the very piece you need to fill that space – this is the best cutting practice of all.

Another possibility, for those who do not feel able to invent designs, is to go to a good source of traditional design and adapt the designs to your purpose.

Most libraries have suitable books on subjects ranging from complex forms of Islamic art to the simplest and most powerful tribal designs.

The design on the coffee table (page 79) is called 'Nishapur' because its theme was taken from a carved plaster panel that came from that part of the Middle East.

The pattern of a round cathedral window could be adapted for mosaic and the design used for the top of a circular coffee table. Nature is an eternal source of marvellous designs. The mosaic table illustrated here, is an example of a natural form stylized for mosaic. A fairly simple project for a beginner would be a mosaic tile based on a sunflower.

It is unlikely that you will be able to cut triangles of exactly the same size.

2a-d. Some of the shapes it is possible to cut by 'nibbling' away the waste.

3a. Once you have spent some time practising cutting shapes you should be left with a selection like the one shown here.

3b. Use these shapes to create a pattern trying out different arrangements.

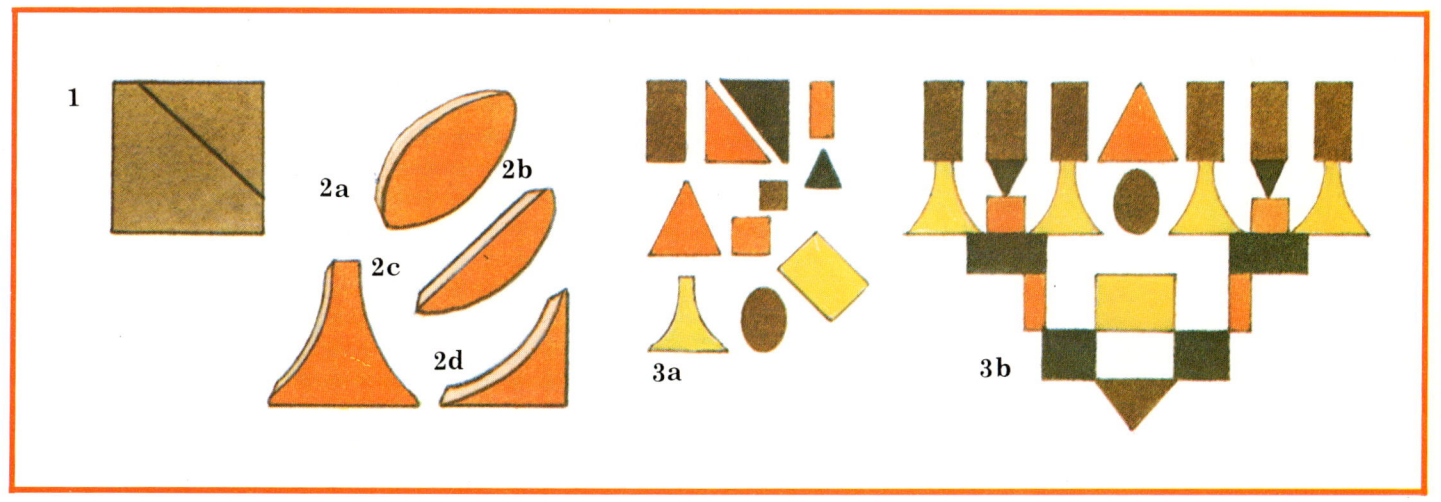

1

2a   2b

2c

2d

3a

3b

The sunflower

Trace the design (fig.4) on to paper using a thick pencil to allow for the cement joins. Leave enough space all round the edge for the paper to be stuck to your working surface.

Stick the paper to the working surface with transparent adhesive tape. It is necessary to secure the paper to the working surface to prevent the design moving around while you work. (For large projects, such as a table top, this is not necessary as the weight of the tesserae keeps the design in place.)

Cut out your shapes. Then stick them to the paper, face downwards and proceed as for the mosaic table.

Edging a round table

You may be lucky enough to find a metal workshop that will make you a metal edging band for a mosaic table. It is then a simple matter to paint it any colour you wish.

Failing this, the usual way to finish a circular mosaic is to clad the side edges with ceramic mosaic which has flat, as distinct from bevelled, edges (fig.5).

Turn your finished mosaic upside down on a large, clean sheet of paper, so that the wood is facing upwards.

Carefully mark out on the paper the spacing for the tesserae (fig.6). By adjusting the spacing you can make sure you use an exact number of tesserae – cut mosaics on the side edge are not a good idea. Never just start sticking and hope it will come out all right.

If your side edge is absolutely smooth stick the ceramic tesserae in place with neat polyvinyl acetate glue.

If, however, the side edge tends to be ragged, use a polyester resin-based, general-purpose repair material – it has more 'body' to fill up the inevitable gaps. (Be sure to get the sort of material which sets very hard – not the elastic sort used for filling dents in motor cars.) A medium-sized tube is ample for most work. If you have never used it before, read the instructions carefully.

After an hour or two, when the material has hardened, turn your table right way up and, with a sharp razor blade, cut off any excess which has stuck to the front of your mosaic.

Tidy up the back before giving it a coat of paint. Then grout the gaps in the side edging with the usual cement and polyvinyl acetate glue mixture.

Small objects

Now that cutting has been tackled you can make small objects for which the full-sized mosaic squares are out of scale.

The most obvious and useful are probably mosaic ashtrays. The

---

4. The trace pattern for the sunflower tile.

one shown here is made from a terracotta flowerpot saucer, filled with a mosaic 'tweed' mixture. To make this it is not necessary to stick your mosaic on to paper first. Simply spread a very stiff mixture of cement and polyvinyl acetate glue (about the consistency of Plasticine) 6mm ($\frac{1}{4}$in) deep in the bottom of your saucer and press the tesserae into it, one at a time.

It will take a little practice to get the surface reasonably level – on the whole it is easiest to start from the middle and work out towards the edge.

A pair of tweezers is very useful – especially for getting out pieces which have sunk, or been buried, in the cement mixture. As soon as the mix seems to have hardened, grout the joins where necessary and clean any cement off the terracotta surround. Unless this cleaning up is done straight away the cement will seep into the porous brick and discolour it.

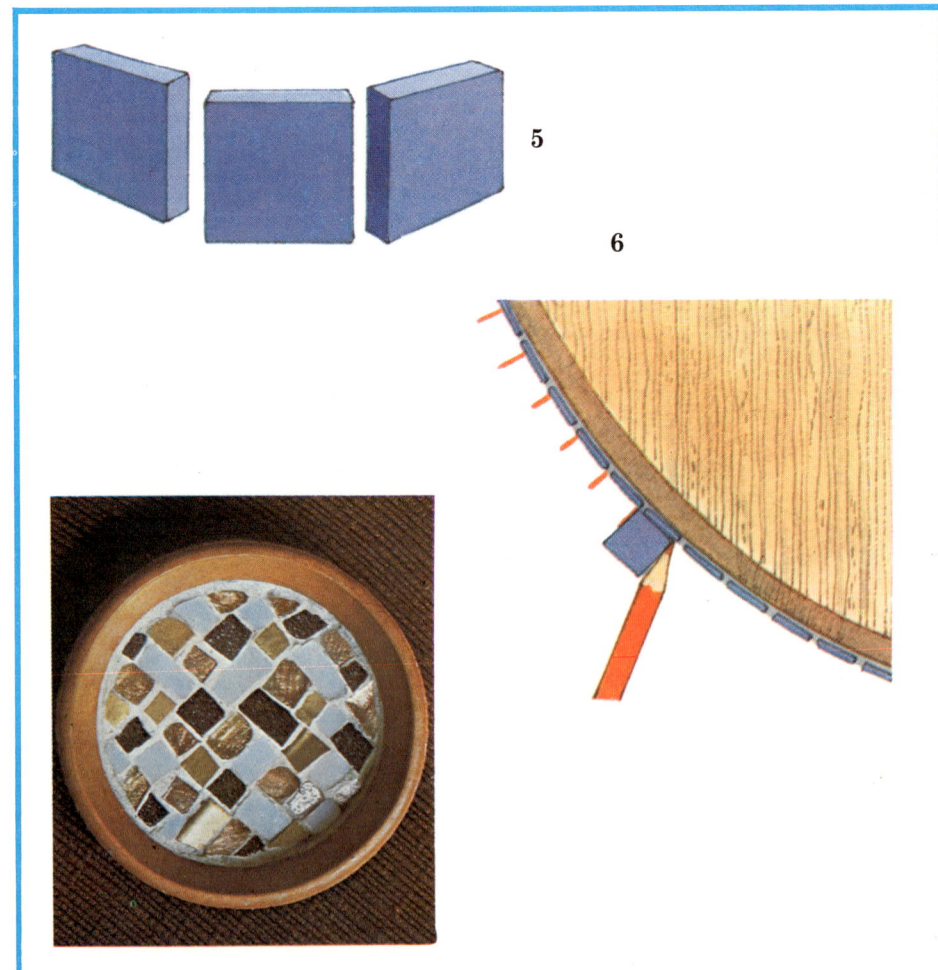

5. Edging tiles have straight edges rather than the normal bevel.
6. Test the spacing of the tesserae until you arrive at an equal spacing which does not require the squares to be cut.
Right: This flower pot saucer has been turned into an attractive ashtray by the addition of a few pieces of mosaic 'tweed' mixture.

Exterior mosaics

The combination of wood and cement plus polyvinyl acetate (PVA) adhesive, though strong and convenient to use indoors, is not really suitable for outdoor use. The contraction and expansion rates of glass, cement and wood when subjected to weeks of rain and frost are so different that sooner or later they will part company. In order to make a tabletop or garden plaque that can be

Left: The mosaic goat can be turned into an attractive wall plaque for the outside of the house by following the directions given here.

left out in all weathers the technique of sand and cement casting has to be mastered.

Beginner's project

It is best to practise the technique on a small scale. All the basic principles can be learnt by working on a mosaic piece no bigger than 15cm (6in) square. The goat (see illustration) can be traced and enlarged straight from the reproduction to make a practice project. Cutting the tesserae for the goat's hair should by now be well within your ability.

Having traced the design, secure the reversed tracing with adhesive tape on to any small piece of plywood you happen to have handy, leaving at least a 2.5cm (1in) surround. Cut and stick mosaic as described on page 80 and page 74.

Casting frame

The casting frame is only a temporary structure to make a neat 2cm ($\frac{3}{8}$in) high wall to hold the cement in place while it sets. It does not have to be an exquisite piece of carpentry, it is essential that you construct the casting frame before mixing the cement. Cut two lengths of batten exactly to size, in this case 15cm (6in). Cut two more lengths of about 18cm (7in) and construct a frame round the mosaic which has an overlap at the corners (fig.1). Bring the lengths of batten as close to the mosaic as possible and use the nails to hold them firm. Bend over the nail heads, or, if they are large enough, drive the nail right down so that the head holds the batten. Do not attempt to nail through the batten or you will split it.

A plaque

It is only worth buying cement and sand by the 50kg (1cwt) bag when you are working on large projects. If you already have some sand that is clean and pebble free this can be used. The proportion of your mix should be two parts sand to one part cement. Contrary to general belief, more cement just weakens the mixture. Before actually mixing the cement check that the chicken wire comfortably fits the casting frame. Ideally do not cement during a heatwave or during frosty weather.

In an old plastic bowl thoroughly mix 1kg (2$\frac{1}{2}$lb) of the sand and cement. Add water a very little at a time and stir constantly. When it looks about the consistency of garden earth after the rain, pick up a handful and squeeze it. If the resultant lump keeps the imprint of your fingers and your squeezing has brought a film of water to the surface, the cement is correctly mixed. Crumbling

---

Plaque

You will need:
Casting frame.
Small bag of ready-mixed sand and cement, about 1kg (2$\frac{1}{2}$lb).
15cm (6in) square of chicken wire.
Hammer.
Palette knife.
Old plastic mixing bowl.
Grease-free wooden spoon.

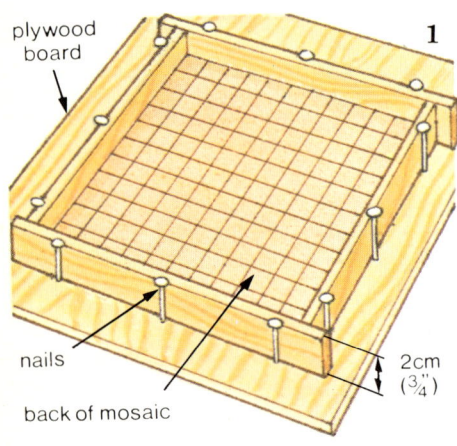

plywood board

1

nails

2cm ($\frac{3}{4}$")

back of mosaic

1. A casting frame is simply constructed using a few pieces of batten held in place with nails. These should be driven home next to the battening, not through it.

cement means it is too dry. Water oozing out between your fingers as you squeeze the cement is an indication that it is too wet.

When you are satisfied with the consistency, start spreading a 6mm ($\frac{1}{4}$in) layer of cement mix on the backs of the mosaic stones with a palette knife. Press well into the joins. Then, with a hammer, very carefully and systematically hammer the cemented surface all over, paying particular attention to the corners. If your hammer begins to pick up lumps of cement mix, dip its head in water and start again. There should be a neat series of pockmarks where you have hammered.

Put the chicken wire into the casting frame next and cover it with the rest of the mix. Fill the casting frame right up to the top and repeat the hammering. Water should rise to the surface from the pressure of the hammering but it should not be oozing out from underneath the frame.

To make the back of the cement level, take another piece of battening, wet it thoroughly under the tap and use it as a straightening edge. Draw it across the top of the cement to remove any excess. Fill any hollows you see with a backwards and forwards motion, till you have a smooth surface. (You may need to wet your batten several times.)

At this point if you intend to hang the plaque outdoors or to fix it permanently to a wall you will need to attach a piece of galvanized wire. Twist it into a loop (fig.2) and bury the straight end well into the cement; at the same time bend the loop at a slight angle so that it stays clear of cement. Cover your work with a plastic sheet and leave it overnight. On no account move it or disturb it in any way; the setting time is really the most delicate stage of the whole operation.

The following day, pour a small cup of water over the cement and cover it again. A hissing sound, as the cement eagerly soaks up the water, indicates your mix was too dry or has set too fast due to very hot weather.

After five days, very cautiously remove the nails and ease the casting frame away from the sides of the mosaic. At this point you will appreciate the reason why the corners were not mitred or joined in any permanent way. Leave the sides to harden overnight, then take a board and turn your work over on to it. Clean off and grout as described on page 76 . If you have done your hammering well, there should be hardly any places that need grouting.

To fix the plaque to a wall, drill a hole and insert the wallplug in the wall, insert the screw with its head protruding about 6mm ($\frac{1}{4}$in). Hang the mosaic from the screw by the wire loop. Once it is hanging mix the plaster of Paris. Start with half a cup of water and,

Fixing the plaque
You will need: A wallplug. A 4cm (1$\frac{1}{2}$in) screw (brass if possible). A small cup of plaster of Paris. Palette knife.

2

2. The wire loop should be twisted to this shape and inserted in the wet cement to hold the plaque.

gradually stirring with a palette knife, add more and more plaster until it is thick and creamy but still pourable.

Holding the mosaic with the bottom against the wall and the top tilted well forward, pour in the plaster of Paris over the loop and screw head. Immediately straighten up the mosaic (plaster sets very fast). It should now be parallel to the wall. Hold it in this position until you can feel it has set.

If it is a rendered wall, the gap between mosaic and wall can be neatly filled with rendering, alternatively a mosaic edge or hardwood frame can be put round it.

A garden table

Having practised on a small scale, you should now be able to tackle a garden table, though there are certain technical differences due to the change of scale.

The actual cementing process will be the same, though this time it will be worthwhile buying a 50kg (1cwt) bag of rendering and cement mix and ask a friend to help with mixing and hammering. The mixing can be very tiring but it is essential that it and the hammering are a continuous process.

You should make the mosaic at least 4cm ($1\frac{1}{2}$in) thick. You will have to reinforce the mosaic with expanded metal. Sheets of this can be bought at most hardware stores. To cut the metal you will need a pair of wire cutters or tin snips.

As the cement depth will be greater, the first layer should be 19mm ($\frac{3}{4}$in) thick, before adding the metal reinforcement. This means the battening will have to be correspondingly deeper, 4cm by 19mm ($1\frac{1}{2}$in by $\frac{3}{4}$in).

The large cement mosaic block will need to dry for two or three weeks and will probably need two people to turn it.

Plaster casting frame

Should you wish to make a round or an oval table, and you cannot find a metal worker to make an iron band for the edging there is a very simple way to make a retaining edge in which to set the cement. This method uses cardboard packets cut into strips 6cm ($2\frac{1}{2}$in) wide, making each one as long as possible. Measure 4cm ($1\frac{1}{2}$in) down the depth of each strip and rule a line.

Bend each cardboard strip along the line to form a right angle. Make angled cuts into the 2.5cm (1in) part of the cardboard strip (fig.3). It is now possible to fit the cardboard round any shape.

Fix the cardboard round the prepared mosaic (which is on a plywood board) and at regular intervals tack it into place.

Mix the plaster of Paris and spread it with a palette knife to cover the tacks right up to the top of the cardboard. Once it has set

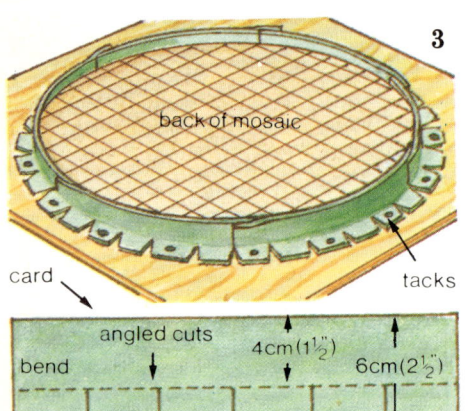

Plaster casting frame

You will need:
Plaster of Paris.
Several old cardboard boxes (cereal boxes are ideal).
Tacks.
Hammer.
Scissors.
Palette knife.
Pencil and ruler.

3

back of mosaic

card   tacks

angled cuts
bend   4cm($1\frac{1}{2}$")   6cm($2\frac{1}{2}$)

3. Circular casting frames are easily made from thin card strips and tacks, the whole thing is then coated with plaster, on the outer edge only, to hold the assembly rigid.

around the cement will be held within a rigid wall. The plaster of Paris is so hard you will have to chisel into it when you want to remove it.

Edging for the table is made from a double row of mosaic to cover the 4cm (1½in) depth. The simplest way to apply it is to buy the ceramic already papered and cut it into 30cm (12in) long strips two stones wide. Spread polyvinyl acetate based filling material a little at a time along the edge and press in the mosaic, paper towards the outside. When set, wash off the paper and grout.

For the base an old sewing machine stand painted white is suitable. For a round table a concrete tube section can be used.

Note: if you live in an area where severe frosts are common it is an advantage to have the top and bottom of the table separate, so the top can be taken off and stored.

Below: An attractive design for a garden table.

Flooring mosaic

It is not advisable for an amateur to attempt to lay an exterior mosaic floor. Levelling the cement bed and making sure that the joins line up is a job demanding a great deal of experience. Glass mosaic is neither strong nor thick enough for flooring. If you have a patio or terrace floor to be covered in mosaic, make a design, paper it up and find a professional tiler to help you lay it. It is advisable to keep your design fairly simple; flooring mosaic is much harder to cut than vitreous mosaic and one can very easily finish with blistered hands.

Pebble mosaic There is, however, a very basic form of flooring mosaic well within your capability – pebble mosaic.

This will make a delightful garden path or cover a bare patch of concrete. Either buy your pebbles by the sack from a gravel pit or, if you live close to the sea, use the pebbles on the beach. The pattern on the pebble mosaic bank illustrated took a week to create. Four sacks of pebbles were used and 152kg (3cwt) of rendering and cement mix.

Sort out pebbles; they should be graded into size and colour. Once you have an idea of what you have you can plan your design. If you can, buy pebbles that are already graded – it is well worth the extra cost.

Before mixing the cement, draw out your whole design on the prepared concrete patch, either using tailor's chalk or diluted paint. Mix the cement a bucket at a time.

Spread one part of the pattern with 2.5cm (1in) thickness of the mixture. Set your pebbles about 2cm ($\frac{3}{4}$in) deep. If they sink right in, the cement mix is too wet. It is best to start in an unimportant corner of the design until you are used to the technique. Try not to get the cement on the top surface of the pebbles as it will spoil the design. At the end of a day's work cut back any cement round the edges so there will be a clean join between one part and the next. Moss will sometimes grow in the joins but this is not always a disadvantage as it can enhance the design.

Again, simple designs are the best especially when using pebbles as no two will be exactly the same. Try to consider the design in terms of shape, size and colour keeping the main areas large with a few focal points of smaller detail to catch the eye. For these, smaller pebbles, preferably of a contrasting colour, should be used. With a little care and forethought you will be able to produce a pebble mosaic to be proud of.

Left: Detail of a pebble mosaic showing the simple, bold style which best suits this type of work.

Plastics

Introducing plastics

Plastic is a lightweight material and is easily worked. It comes in liquid form as a polyester resin or it can be solid such as acrylic plastic. It is either poured or cut accordingly. Plastic is at its best when transparent or translucent. Unlike glass, it does not simply let light pass through it but diffuses it and carries it along its length, even round curves in a rod, to give the edge a fluorescent light. You can make all sorts of beautiful, modern designs in plastic, such as chess pieces, paper weights, jewelry, door knobs, magazine racks and trays.

If you think of plastic only as a substitute for materials such as glass, wood or metal, then reconsider. Plastic comes in an exciting variety of forms and colours and behaves in a completely different way from any other material.

Plastic is made up of chemicals derived from coal and petroleum and this chemical structure can be altered to suit different purposes. Plastic is really a collective word for a number of materials, many quite unlike one another. They can, however, be divided into two main groups.

Thermoplastics

These are plastics which are hard at normal temperatures but soften when heated. The temperature needs to be controlled to prevent the plastic from bubbling and therefore shrinking. The material can be shaped and moulded and will retain the new shape when it cools to its former solid mass. The process can be repeated a number of times before the material starts to break down.

Acrylic in sheets or rods, celluloid, expanded polystyrene (EPS) and polyvinyl chloride (PVC) are all examples of thermoplastics.

Thermosetting plastics

These are a group of materials that undergo a chemical change which is irreversible. They solidify in the presence of heat and, once shaped and cooled, they cannot be reworked. They can be reinforced with glass fibre which makes them strong enough to be used for structural purposes.

Polyester resin

Polyester resin is a liquid which solidifies by a chemical reaction when a catalyst is added. An accelerator is also needed to help speed up the curing process; most resins are already accelerated by the manufacturer. Once the catalyst is added, the accelerated resin produces heat and starts to polymerize or cure. It turns from a liquid to a jelly, then to a soft but solid state and finally very hard. Resins can be coloured with pigments, used with metal fillers and reinforced with glass fibre to make a very strong, resilient material. There are a number of different kinds of polyester resins suitable for craft work. Although there are several distinguishable categories of resin each manufacturer introduces slight variations in a 'mix' and calls a resin by a different brand name. Because of these variations it is wise to use the same manufacturer's products for any one project.

If you are in any doubt as to the type of resin you need for a particular project it is advisable to ask your craft shop or manufacturer for advice. Most manufacturers will be happy to supply these details and some publish explanatory leaflets on their products.

Types of polyester resin

Embedding resin is a clear resin for embedding objects, either for their decorative effect or to preserve them. It has a long cure time, low exotherm (heat) and low shrinkage. It can be cast in large blocks.

Rigid laminating resin is a general-purpose resin, clear mauve in colour and suitable for most kinds of resin and glass fibre projects. It can be used in conjunction with resin pigments and fillers.

Thixotropic paste is a very thick resin which is normally added to other laminating resins to make them thicker. When used on its own for patching and gluing an accelerator must be added.

Gel coat resin is a laminating resin with the addition of thixotropic paste. It is used on sloping surfaces and for impregnation of all glass fibre reinforcements.

Flexible resin is added to a laminating resin where solid blocks or

---

Safety hints

Take care: some plastics are inflammable, some fumes are toxic, and some may irritate the skin. However, they are perfectly safe to work with in the home if you take the following simple precautions. Store all plastic materials in a cool, dark place.

The room in which you are working must be warm and well ventilated. This is important because resin fumes can be toxic.

Do not smoke when working with plastics and do not work in a room where there is an open flame.

Keep materials away from food.

Avoid contact with the eyes.

If you find it difficult to work wearing rubber gloves use a protective cream on the hands.

Work on a heat resistant surface that has been covered with newspaper.

Use disposable containers for mixing resin and do not throw away the excess until it has cooled down.

Wear old clothing and remove any spilt resin with acetone.

Should your skin come into contact with the resin wash it immediately with cold water.

Wipe up any spilt resin with a paper towel and dispose of it – do not use it a second time.

Dispose of all cleaning materials and waste as soon as you have finished working with the resin.

slabs are to be cast. The heat of the exotherm creates stresses in blocks of resin: flexible resin helps to disperse the stresses and so prevents cracking.

Clear cast embedding

Embedding is the process whereby an object is surrounded by a solid mass of resin. This is usually done in two layers for a single object, or in a number of layers, depending on the number of objects and the way they are spaced. Each layer is known as a 'pour'. The first pour is to create the outer surface and to support the object. The second pour is to cover the object, thus embedding it. There is no end to the things that can be embedded in resin. The casts you make can be varied not only by the object you embed but also by the shape of the mould and the colour of the resin. You can tint the resin slightly for a special effect, or make the back or base of the mould an opaque colour as a background. You can

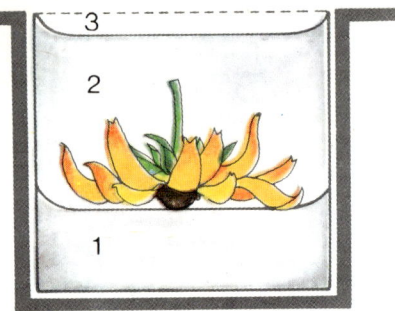

Above: Three stages in embedding an object. If using a flower, it is good practice to dip the specimen in resin before beginning the second pour to prevent air bubbles forming in the cast.
Right: A selection of materials and tools required for embedding.
Right: Almost any object is suitable for embedding as long as it is completely dry.

make paper weights, buttons, door knobs, jewelry, key rings, picture mounts, chess and backgammon pieces – in fact you can apply this technique to most objects.

Experiment with embedding dried flowers and grasses, some of which are more suitable than others. The colour tends to fade–red more so than yellow – but artificial flowers can be embedded successfully.

You can embed coins, insects, colourful seeds, coloured glass chips, watch parts, unusual stamps, address cards and shells. You can also make large clear blocks to mount or to set photographs in. It is important to remember that whatever you embed must be free of moisture.

The process is easy and you do not require any special tools. The materials are easily available and for a high gloss finish the cast can be polished with a metal polish. Resins can be purchased from hobby shops or manufacturers in various quantities. Buy the appropriate catalyst at the same time. You can buy an embedding kit or you can buy the resin and catalyst separately.

Making a cast

Cover working surface with newspaper. Lay out all tools and equipment. Some moulds are marked with their capacity but, if not, fill mould with water up to the level required for the first pour – usually $\frac{1}{2}$ to $\frac{1}{3}$ the total depth of cast. Pour the water into a measuring jug to find the capacity. If you do not want to mix the resin and catalyst in the measuring jug, pour the water into a paper cup and mark the water level. Dry the mould and the paper cup thoroughly.

Polish the mould with wax polish which helps to release the cast. If you want to make more than one cast prepare the moulds together.

Remember that the open end of the mould will usually be the back or bottom of the object you are making. The smooth inside surface of the mould will form the outside surface of the cast.

Measure out the resin and add the appropriate amount of catalyst, following manufacturer's instructions.

The catalyst bottle is marked with quantity guidelines which will tell you how much catalyst to add, and the bottle is fitted with a pinhole bung which makes dropping easier and more precise. If you want to tint the cast, add the pigment before you add the catalyst and mix it well – stirring slowly to avoid trapping air bubbles.

Once the catalyst has been added, stir the mixture slowly for a minute before carefully pouring it into the mould.

A cast

You will need:
Clear cast resin.
Catalyst or hardener.
Mould.
Object to embed.
Paper cups.
Measuring jug.
Smooth stick or flat wooden spoon.
Wax polish.
Chrome or metal polish.
Pigments (optional).
Felt (optional).
A cleaner such as a polyester resin solvent or a concentrated resin detergent for cleaning utensils. (Do not let this come into contact with your skin. If it does, wash off immediately.)
Newspaper.

Right: The various stages in embedding an object. (left to right) Applying release agent to the mould. Measuring the resin. Adding the catalyst. Mix the catalyst into the resin carefully to prevent the formation of air bubbles. Making the first pour, again slowly to prevent air bubbles. The object is then placed in position and the final pour made. Carefully remove the cast from the mould and finally finish the sticky surface with wet and dry abrasive paper.

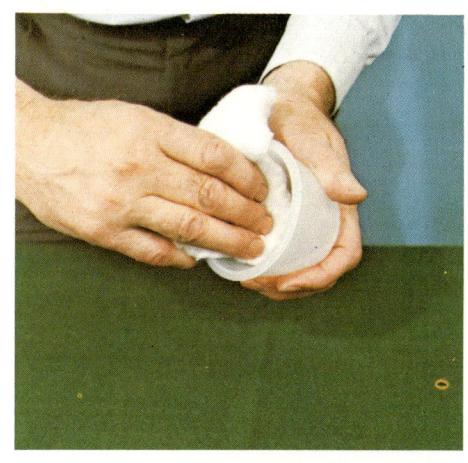

Set the mould aside on a level surface and cover it lightly with foil to prevent the surface from collecting dust. You can place the mould at an angle if you want a sloping surface.

Leave the cast for about three hours or until it has gelled. The length of time can vary depending on the amount of catalyst used.

Embedding an object

Some objects are inclined to trap air when being embedded. If you are using a coin, prepare it by pouring a few drops of resin mixed with catalyst on to the face. Leave to set and place this side down on the gel before the second pour. Address cards can be treated in the same way. Dried flowers should be immersed in resin before being embedded.

Place the object upside down on the tacky surface of the first pour. If the object is very light in weight you can coat it with a clear plastic adhesive to keep it in position. Once this has dried, make the second pour.

The sticky surface of the cast can be covered with a piece of felt or you can cover it with a thin layer of resin to which you have added more than the usual amount of catalyst. This will cure to a smooth finish.

The resin can take several hours to cure completely, depending on the brand of resin and the size of the cast.

Removing the cast

If a cast is difficult to remove from a mould, immerse it in cold water and bring to the boil. Then plunge it in cold water. If it still sticks repeat the process – it will work.

Rub the cast down with a metal polish for a highly polished finish. You can also rub it down with a fine silicon carbide paper and then use a metal polish, but this is difficult to do by hand and requires a lot of practice. If you do attempt it, try it out on a small test cast first.

Once you have made a few casts you will find it easy to make larger objects and to adapt the technique to a wide range of articles.

Patience is essential for good results. Satisfy your initial enthusiasm by making small casts – larger casts take a long time to cure. But even when making small casts, apply the following hints – they will improve your casts and make the whole process easier when you attempt larger pieces.

The object to be embedded must be dry and free of dust.

Avoid trapping bubbles by stirring the resin slowly.

The percentage of catalyst used must be decreased as the amount of

Above: Dust, moisture and trapped air bubbles are the problems most commonly experienced by the beginner.

resin to be poured is increased. Too much catalyst will form cracks in the cast – although you might do this for special effects. The amount of heat generated is relative to the amount of catalyst used, so if an excessive amount of catalyst is used not only will it form cracks in the cast but it can also ruin the mould. Alternatively, large moulds can be filled in several pours. It is better to use too little catalyst than too much. The surface can always be cured artificially if necessary by applying a thin coat of resin to which a larger proportion of catalyst has been added. You can also use this method to join a base to the sticky surface of the cast.

Store the resin containers in a cool, dark place and cover them so that they do not collect dust. Dust could fall into the resin when you pour it from the container, so work in a dust-free atmosphere and cover the casts while curing.

Manufactured and home-made moulds

When casting objects that do not need the optical clarity of clear-cast embedding, you can use ordinary casting resin. This can be coloured in any opaque colour or it can be finished and stained once the cast has cured. Depending on the object being cast and the required weight, the resin can be used either with a filler, to give it weight, or without if it does not need to be heavy.

A filler is a material used to give a cast weight, to cut down on the amount of resin used, or to give it a metallic appearance. If the cast is to be opaque then a filler can be used, as no optical or translucent qualities are required. The filler can be up to 50% of the total volume to be cast.

You can use a metallic powder filler especially made for this purpose which gives the appearance of copper, iron or brass. Alternatively, you can use fine sand, flour, plaster of Paris, metal filings, glass fibre, talc, powdered slate or chalk. Different fillers will give you various textured finishes so you can experiment with small pieces until you get the particular results you want.

The cast can be coloured when you have mixed the resin and the filler but before you add the catalyst. Any of the colour pigments made for resin can be used. Black and ivory – which give a very natural colour – work particularly well. Once the casts have cured you can use any wood stain or household paint to 'antique' the cast. Cover the cast with the stain or paint and, while it is still wet, rub the paint from the more prominent surfaces and leave to dry.

Manufactured moulds

Special-purpose moulds obtainable from craft shops generally come in four types.

Above: Another problem sometimes confronting the beginner, too much catalyst causes cracking due to the stress created by the resin setting too quickly.

Flexible moulds such as rubber moulds for candle making, plaster casting or resin casting are probably the most versatile. Semi-flexible polythene moulds are used for clear-cast resin and candle making.

Two-part moulds, usually produced by vacuum forming, are used for all types of materials but the range of available moulds is limited.

Rigid moulds such as ceramic, metal and glass offer a high degree of surface polish and therefore lend themselves especially well to resin casting.

Manufactured moulds can be bought from craft shops or manufacturers in many different forms. You can buy moulds to make chess pieces, candles, pendants and a variety of objects.

Although a bought mould will not give you an original design you can make it look different by giving it an antique appearance or by staining it. These moulds will give you some experience in casting more intricate pieces before you actually start making your own moulds.

Once the moulds have been filled with resin they will have to be supported until they have cured. There are two ways in which this may be done.

If the filler you have used is not heavy you can suspend the moulds in a piece of cardboard which has a hole cut into it to fit the base of the mould. If the filler is heavy this method might stretch the mould or pull it out of shape. To avoid this, hold the mould in a paper cup, slightly larger than the mould, and fill surrounding area with rice or fine sand.

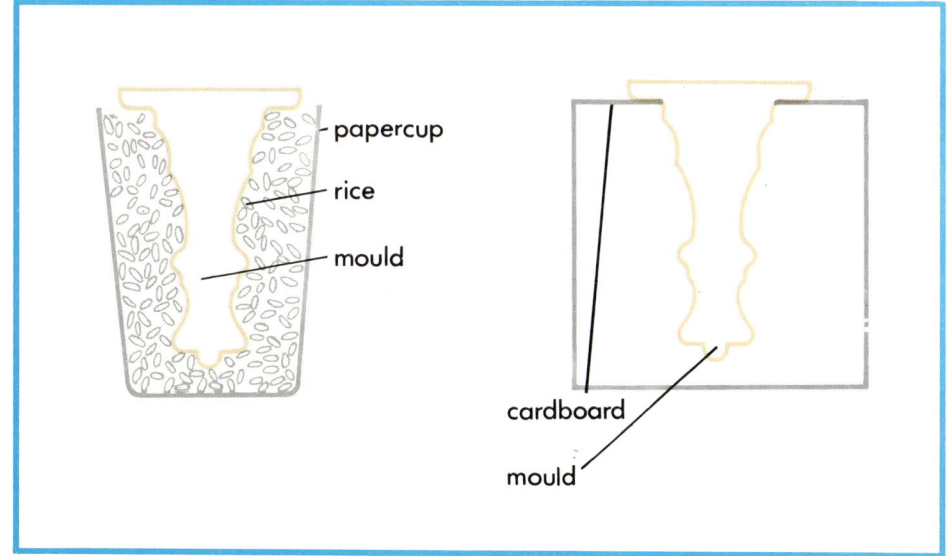

Far left: This picture frame was cast using a commercial mould.
Above: Resin chess pieces can be made in any desired colour simply by the addition of pigment to the resin before pouring.
Left: In order to prevent the mould distorting under the weight of the resin, it should be stood in a container surrounded by rice or sand or alternatively suspended from its base.

101

Chessmen

Prepare a working area in a well-ventilated room. Lay down news paper. Work out the quantity of resin and filler you will need (see page 96).

If you are using a manufacturer's resin, filler and moulds, they usually include the capacity of the moulds. Of the total quantity required, use about 60% resin and 40% filler.

Mix the resin and the filler by stirring in small quantities of the filler until it has dispersed in the resin.

Either use two different colours of pigment or paint one of the sets on completion.

Add the colour pigment, if required, and thoroughly mix the resin. The red and green chessmen were coloured in this manner. Leave the resin mixture to stand for a few minutes so that any trapped air bubbles can rise to the surface. Add the catalyst or hardener to the mixture and stir it carefully to avoid making air bubbles.

Half fill the mould and allow the mixture to flow around the entire surface of the mould by tilting and flexing the mould with thumb and forefinger. This will ensure that all the detail is impressed and it also helps to prevent trapping air.

Suspend the mould from cardboard or pack it into a paper cup and fill the sides with rice.

Fill the mould with the resin mixture and leave it to cure. Curing time will vary depending on room temperature and the type of resin used.

When the mould is completely dry peel back a corner and wash the entire mould in washing-up liquid. Continue peeling back the mould until the original is released.

If you prefer you can shake some talc on to the mould and then peel it back. Always support the mould when casting to prevent it from stretching and losing its shape.

If there are small imperfections caused by air bubbles in the cast you can mix a small amount of resin and catalyst and use a match-stick to apply it to the cast. Once it is dry the appearance will be perfect.

You can stain or paint the piece if you did not use colour pigment. In either case the finished piece may be 'antiqued' by the method described on page 99 .

If you glue a piece of felt to the bottom of the cast then you will not have to worry about the sticky surface. Alternatively, sand down this part of the cast with moistened silicon carbide paper.

Making your own moulds

Both flexible and rigid moulds can be made at home using a

Chessmen

You will need:
Clear cast resin.
Catalyst or hardener.
Filler.
Moulds.
Paper cups.
Measuring jug.
Smooth stick or flat wooden spoon.
Pigment (optional).
Felt (optional).
Rice or cardboard for suspending moulds.
Fine silicon carbide paper (optional).
Chrome or metal polish (optional).
Resin cleaner for utensils.
(Caution: do not get this on your skin.)
Newspaper.

variety of materials. The object to be repeated is called the master; a mould is shaped round the master and the repeat, or replica, made in the mould is called the cast (fig.1).

The master can be used for casting wax, resin or plaster. When choosing a master, thought must be given to the function of the cast. For example, if you are using resin to make a paper-weight you will need a master with at least one flat surface to form the open end of the mould and then the base.

The mould should be impervious i.e. it should hold the casting liquid without leaking.

The second requirement is that you must be able to remove the master. Sometimes this means you will need to make the mould in more than one piece as with a solid plaster of Paris mould.

If you want to be able to re-use the mould it must either be flexible or made in two or more sections. Failing this you must choose a shape which allows the cast to slip out easily, in which case it must be wide at the open end with no undercuts (fig.2). A rough-textured mould, particularly when there are undercuts or variations in thickness, will not part as willingly with its cast as a perfectly smooth, even-surfaced mould.

Textured moulds may not be suitable for clear-cast resin as you will lose the optical clarity but, if you are using an opaque resin, with or without colour and or filler, then the textural possibilities are endless.

Any items that have a shape suited to your requirements can be used as moulds. Even such apparently unlikely objects as pots, eggshells and electric lightbulbs have been used successfully for casting clear resin. However, in these instances, it is necessary to destroy the mould to release the cast. Flexible polythene containers, used for a variety of household products, make excellent moulds and usually have a very suitable surface. However, they may require cutting with a trimming knife to remove unwanted features.

If you do use household objects remember that, if you are casting resin, the mould must be capable of withstanding the heat generated while curing.

There are a number of traditional materials used for making moulds. Any clay-like material can be used to shape an original mould. Clay, when fired (glazed or unglazed) and plaster of Paris are suitable for all kinds of casting. Synthetic and air-drying clays and chemical compounds which dry very hard can also be used as they are unaffected by heat. But modelling materials, such as Plasticine, can be affected by heat and are best used with cold-setting materials only.

1 master mould

casts

2 wrong right

1. *The original is known as the master. It is used to make the mould which is used in turn to make the casts – exact replicas of the original.*
2. *Not all objects are suitable as masters using the techniques described here.*

Above: A selection of moulds for resin casting.

There are a number of materials which can be used to give a mould with an irregular shape. For example you can use kitchen foil to make candle-holders from clear-cast resin. If you crumple the kitchen foil and then shape it, the cast made from it will have a rough crystal appearance. Similarly, cellophane paper can be used to embed candy, to look like the original packet which they were in. The master must be dry and free from grease. Wash it in soapy water and then dry it thoroughly.

Re-meltable rubber moulds

Re-meltable rubber can be extremely useful because the mould can either be used a number of times or melted down to make a new mould.

The easiest way to make a mould is to hold the object with tweezers or tongs and to dip it into the melted rubber. This method is only suitable if the master has an existing base that will give the cast a firm, flat surface to rest on.

Heat the rubber over a low heat in an old saucepan. Take care not to spill any of the rubber and do not overheat it. Once it has melted it is ready for use.

Using tweezers or tongs, grip the object close to the base or around the base and dip it into the rubber.

Swirl it around slightly to release any bubbles that might be trapped around the object.

Remove from the rubber and let it cool for a few minutes.

Dip it into the rubber a second time and remove it. Do not leave it in the rubber too long or the first layer may melt.
Let the second layer cool. The mould should be about 3mm ($\frac{1}{8}$in)

Re-meltable rubber mould

You will need:
A master from which to make the mould.
Re-meltable rubber.
Plasticine or clay to shape the base, if one is required.
An old saucepan.
Tweezers or tongs if dipping or brush if painting.
Scissors.
Sugar thermometer.
Newspaper.
Kitchen foil.

Left: To make a mould from an existing object the master requires a base which should be made of clay or Plasticine. When melting the rubber, be careful not to overheat it as it is a highly inflammable material. Paint the master with the rubber and allow to cool. It will be necessary to apply two or three coats to build up a suitable thickness of rubber. When cool the mould is simply peeled off the master.

thick so, if it appears thin, dip it a third time. If you let the first two coats cool sufficiently the mould should now be strong enough to use. If it still looks flimsy, dip it again. Leave to cool for a couple of hours so that it is completely set.

If the shape of the master does not lend itself to the dipping technique you can paint it instead. First make a base for the master. This will also give the necessary 'lip' to support the mould when you are casting.

Flatten a piece of clay or Plasticine until it is slightly larger than the bottom of the object. Place the master on the clay lightly, so that the melted rubber will not seep below the master.

Using the clay or Plasticine build up a low wall around the object. Paint the melted rubber into all the little crevices of the object and make sure you get an even coating. Let this coat cool before applying more rubber. Wash the brush with hot water and soap after each coating otherwise it will be ruined.

If the master is very tall, with steep sides, the rubber will tend to run off it so start from the top and work down. Finish off by giving the top an extra coating.

Once the rubber has set, cut away the rough edges along the bottom with a pair of scissors. Remember that you can melt this down and reuse it later.

Cold rubber moulds

If the master you want to use for making a mould will not stand up to the heat of melted rubber then you can use a cold latex solution instead. This material cannot be re-melted to make more moulds but you can make any number of casts from one mould. Stand the master on a piece of cardboard slightly larger than the base.

Paint the liquid latex on to the master and paint a small surround on the cardboard. This will form the 'lip' from which the mould is suspended when making a cast.

Brush away all air-bubbles and leave until dry to touch. Wash the brush in cold water to prevent the bristles from sticking together. In a mixing bowl, or other container, mix enough filler with the latex rubber to give a creamy consistency. The filler strengthens the mould and helps build up the thickness more quickly. Paint the mixture on to the master and leave to dry overnight. Place near a radiator or in a warm cupboard to speed up the process.

The mould should now be thick enough to remove. If the master is large, the mould might require another coating with the latex and filler mixture.

Leave to dry. Remove mould from master using the method described on page 102.

Cold rubber mould

You will need:
A master from which to make the mould.
Cold latex liquid.
Filler.
Brush.
Cardboard.
Old mixing bowl.
Newspaper.

Making a tabletop and window box

Polyester resin is such a versatile material that, as well as being cast and embedded, it can also be used to coat a surface. You can make a light, translucent tabletop using plate glass for the base; this is covered with layers of resin and placed into a table frame. The technique used is so flexible that it can be applied to any flat glass or acrylic sheet. You could try this method for a window or screen.

Wood can also be coated with polyester resin and embedded with nails or other interesting objects to make a bas-relief panel.

Tabletop

Cover an even, flat surface with newspaper and set out all the tools and materials. Wipe over the glass with a cloth dipped in white spirit or paint thinner to remove all dirt and grease. Tape the masking tape round the perimeter of the glass and make sure that it sticks under the glass to give a tight seal (fig.1). The tape prevents the resin from running off the glass.

With a calibrated cup, measure 225gm (8oz) resin into a tin. Add one of the pigments a little at a time. Stir gently but well. If you are mixing up several shades of one colour mix the lightest shade first. In any case start with a light colour just to get the feel of how much colour is needed.

Add 200 drops of catalyst. The catalyst bottle is marked with quantity guidelines to help you. At average room temperature, 19°C (67°F), the pot life of catalysed resin is about 25 minutes. The addition of colour may change the pot life by a few minutes. Pour the resin on to the glass, streaking it up and down its length.

Tabletop
You will need: One sheet of plate glass 46cm by 92cm (1½ft by 3ft). Plate glass is thicker than ordinary window glass. Metal table frame to take panel 46cm by 92cm (1½ft by 3ft). 1kg (2lb) clear embedding resin. Catalyst, which usually comes in 56g (2oz) bottles. You will need 56g (2oz) for the table. Two or three transparent resin pigments. About 3m (3yd) of 2.5cm (1in) wide masking tape. Three large tins for mixing the resin. Measuring jug. Paper cups. Smooth stick or flat wooden spoon. Small sharp knife. White spirit or paint thinner. Resin cleaner for utensils (do not get on skin). Medium and fine silicon carbide paper. Chrome or metal polish. Newspaper.

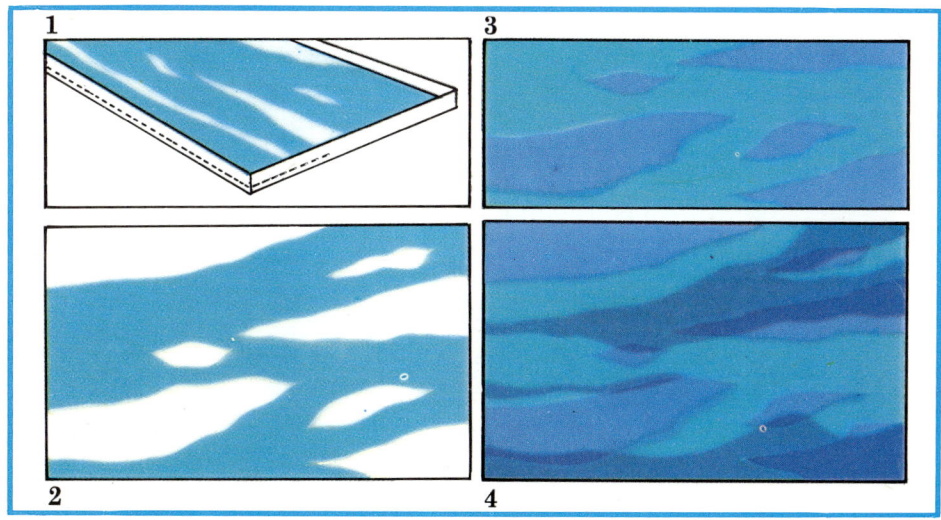

1. Having made a wall around the glass, pour the first colour and leave to gel.
2. Before the resin sets, cut away the areas not required.
3. After the second pour, the resin may again be cut away.
4. Finally the third pour is made.

The resin will spread out and find its own level.

Wait for the resin to become a jelly (about four to five hours). Then, using the knife, cut out any shapes you wish from the resin and lift from the glass (fig.2). Start by cutting out flowing shapes. You will find that the resin peels off the glass easily at this stage. Mix up another 225g (8oz) of resin with another colour and catalyse in the same way as before.

Pour on to the glass in a second layer. Once the first layer has set the two resins will not mix (fig.3). When the second layer has gelled (about four to five hours) you can again cut and peel away portions of the resin. You may like to leave one or two 'peep-holes' of plain glass uncovered by resin.

Mix up third 225g (8oz) resin with another colour and catalyst. Pour and cut in the same way as before (fig.4). The last 225g (8oz) of resin can be made by mixing two of the pigments together. The table shown has only three layers of resin but you can add a fourth if you wish. Be sparing, however, with darker colours until you have some experience of working with resin. The darker colours can easily swamp the lighter shades.

Leave the tabletop to completely cure and harden overnight or longer if possible. Make sure it is not sticky to the touch.

When you are sure that it is hard, peel off the tape and rub over the resin with dampened medium and fine silicon carbide paper. Follow by buffing with chrome or metal polish.

Place the tabletop glass side uppermost in a metal-framed coffee table unit. These units can be bought as a simple metal frame into which the top can easily be slotted.

Window box

Resin can be embedded with a variety of nails to make an attractive window box like the one illustrated here. You can add texture to any flat surface to create panels, plaques or tiles. Found objects such as a length of chain, a horseshoe or shells make a design which is durable, looks chunky and gives an interesting texture.

The resin you need is a general-purpose polyester resin, pre-accelerated and pale mauve in colour. It can be coloured with a number of resin pigments, used with metal fillers or made up of a mixture of half resin and half sand.

Lay cut newspaper on a working surface and set out all the tools and materials.

Design an arrangement of nails to go on the blockboard. Lightly hammer the heads of the nails into the wood so they stand clear of the surface of the wood. The intention is to hold the nails steady until the resin sets. Some nails will be lying flat in your

---

Window box

You will need:
A piece of blockboard 77cm by 23cm (2ft 6in by 9in) and 13mm ($\frac{1}{2}$in) thick.
340g (12oz) general purpose polyester resin.
Catalyst.
56g (2oz) metal filler.
About 56g (2oz) each of carpet tacks and thin 2.5cm (1in) nails, and half a dozen flooring nails.
Strip of cardboard 5cm (2in) wide and 2m (6ft 6in) long.
Masking tape.
Large can or metal bucket.
Measuring jug.
Paper cups.
Smooth stick or flat wooden spoon.
Small soft brush (such as old pastry brush).
Small or medium hammer.
Sandpaper.
Polyurethane varnish (optional).
Resin cleaner for utensils (do not get on skin).
Newspaper.

Left: The completed tabletop is fixed in a frame to finish the coffee table.

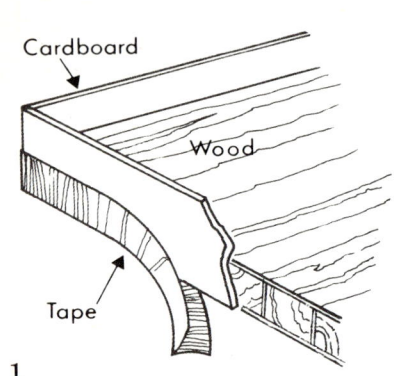

1

Above right: The completed window box.

1. Make a seal around the edges of the front panel using card and masking tape making sure that the seal is tight.

design and you do not need to hammer these.

Cut the strip of cardboard into lengths equal to the four sides of the piece of blockboard. The cardboard strips will prevent the resin from running over the edge of the board. Tape the strips round the edges of the board, making sure that the tape extends underneath the board for a firm hold and tight seal (fig. 1).

Using a calibrated cup measure 340g (12oz) resin into the tin. Add the catalyst. You will need about 70 drops of catalyst. Working quickly, but without rushing, spoon out the mixture onto the board and spread out evenly to get a smooth layer. Any objects which have not already been hammered on to the board should be arranged at this stage.

When the resin is at the jelly stage (four to five hours) sprinkle the metal filler over the surface. Spread it evenly and as quickly as you like. Any excess can be brushed off later.

Wait for the resin to harden overnight, or longer if possible. When the resin has hardened, brush the excess filler off with a pastry brush. Brush thoroughly round all the nails. Wrap the fragments in newspaper and put in the waste bin.

Remove the cardboard strips.

If the window box is going to be out of doors you can varnish the front panel with a clear polyurethane varnish for extra protection. To convert the panel into a window box add two sides, a bottom and a back panel of blockboard. Sand down the wood and varnish for a good finish. You will have an attractive and sturdy container for your plants.

Working with glass fibre

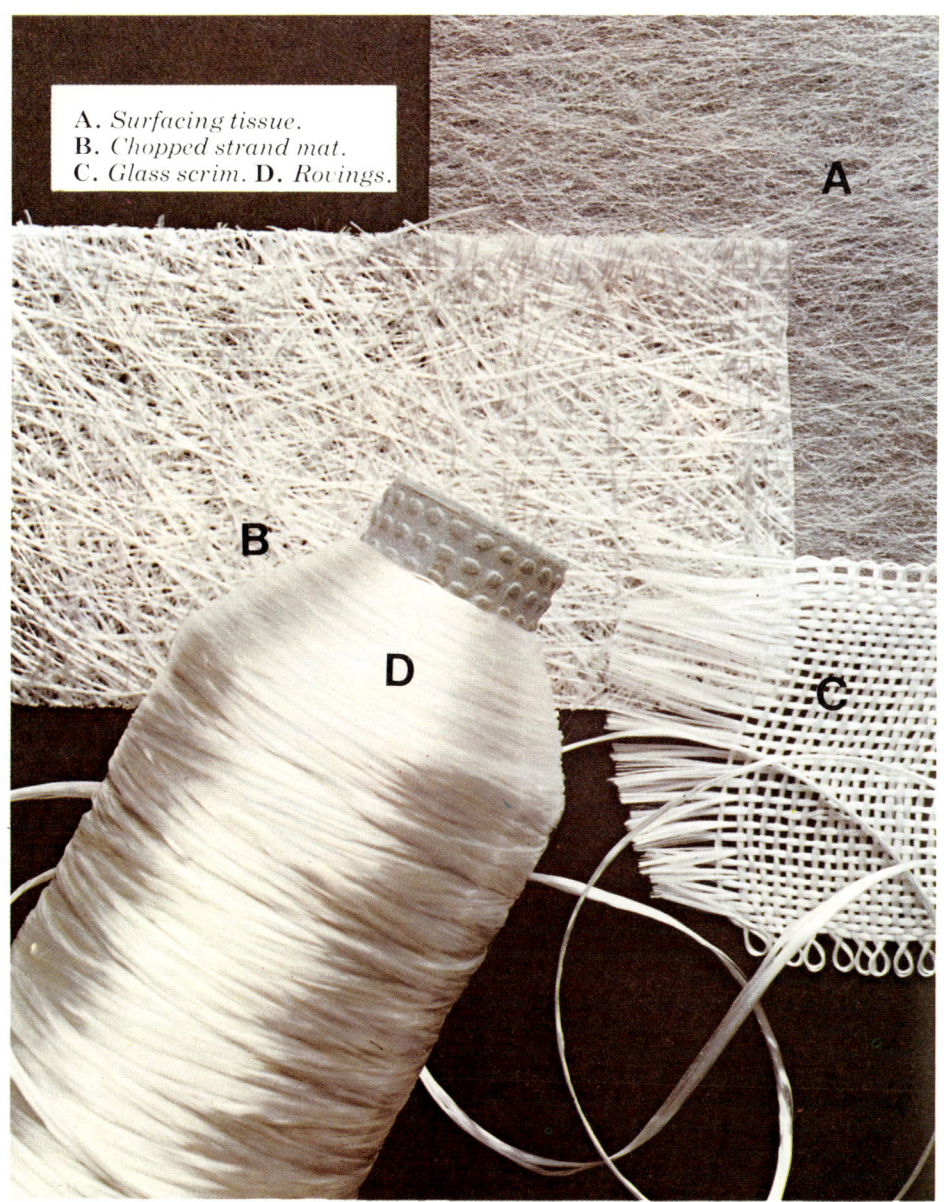

A. *Surfacing tissue.*
B. *Chopped strand mat.*
C. *Glass scrim.* D. *Rovings.*

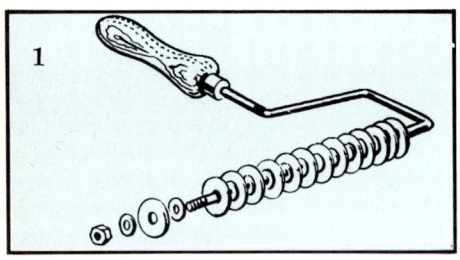

1

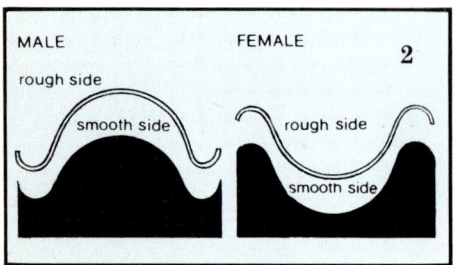

MALE   FEMALE   2
rough side
smooth side
rough side
smooth side

Polyester resin is used to make a variety of craft objects, both decorative and practical. The resin on its own, however, is not very strong; it needs the introduction of glass fibre to make a tough, almost indestructible material, strong enough for car bodies, simple enough to use at home and sufficiently versatile to make a tray, lampshade or screen.

Resin-impregnated glass fibre cloth laid in layers over a mould is known as a laminate. The first layer of resin which provides the smooth top surface is called the gel coat. Two or more layers of impregnated glass fibre are later added. When cured the object is separated from its mould and is extremely durable and lightweight. This type of material, sometimes called glass fibre-reinforced plastic (GRP), can be sawn, drilled or joined together and, in addition, it can be easily repaired if damaged.

Glass fibre is usually 90cm (1yd) wide and can be purchased by a measured amount or by the roll. It is generally priced by weight.

Surfacing tissue is a very fine material used to cover a rough surface of glass fibre when it needs to be extra smooth.

Chopped strand mat is most often used for reinforcing resin. The fibres are laid in all directions and it is easy to tease out some of the mat to join it to another cut section.

Glass scrim is like a cloth which can easily be laid into deep curves. It is used instead of chopped strand mat when the mould has a deep or intricate curvature.

Rovings are filaments of glass plaited into a cord. The rovings are the basic yarn used to make the various glass fibre cloths.

Making a glass fibre tray

If you have worked with polyester resins before you will be familiar with many of the materials and techniques used to make a glass fibre tray.

Open the windows to ventilate the room. Lay newspaper over and around the working surface and have all the materials, tools and equipment to hand.

Put on an overall or apron and cover skin with protective cream. The mould can be one of two types as shown in fig.2. The negative or female mould is recessed and used for articles that need to be finished or smooth on the convex side. The positive or male mould is domed and the finished side is on the concave surface of the shell. In this case the existing tray is used as a master from which a male mould is produced (i.e. the inside of the tray is coated with glass fibre). If by good fortune your chosen tray is the same design top and bottom you can use it as a male mould without having to make another initial mould. If you do this, halve the quantities of materials needed for the tray.

Of course, once you have made a male mould you can use it again and again to make as many trays as you want.

Wash the tray in warm water and detergent and dry thoroughly. If the tray is made of a porous material seal the upper surface with a thin coat of varnish. Be meticulous about covering the whole surface otherwise the release agent will soak into the tray and the glass fibre will stick.

Sparingly apply the emulsion wax over the upper surface of the tray. Add a little water to the wax if necessary to make it spread more evenly. After the wax has dried, polish with a soft cloth until all swirl marks are removed and the surface has become smooth and shiny.

If the tray is being used for the first time as a mould apply at least three coats of wax allowing two hours between each coat and polishing each time. Every time the tray is used as a mould you should polish (but not wax) to make the surface smooth. Once the wax has dried it is hard and waterproof.

After wax polishing, apply a coat of polyvinyl acetate (PVA) release agent using a small sponge. The wax surface must be protected every time the tray is used as a mould by a thin coat of polyvinyl acetate (PVA); apply in a dust-free atmosphere otherwise small specks will show up on the finished mould. Every part of the upper surface of the tray should be covered otherwise you may have difficulty in removing the mould. Using a brush apply a thin layer of resin to the tray. The gel coat should be about 3mm ($\frac{1}{8}$in) thick.

Measure 226g (8oz) of resin. Add the pigment to the resin, a little at a time, until you find the right depth of colour. This stage is not strictly necessary when making a mould but it will give you practice in mixing the pigment and this will be useful when you make the actual tray.

Add the catalyst, 9 to 10 drops per 28g (1oz). If in doubt as to the amount of catalyst to use follow the manufacturer's instructions. Apply the catalyzed resin to the inside of the tray in a thin, smooth coat. Use a laminating brush or paint brush and wash the brush in resin cleaner or detergent after use. The resin should gel in about an hour given average room temperature, 19°C (67°F).

Cut two pieces of chopped strand mat and one piece of surfacing tissue (not strictly necessary for the mould) equal to the area of the tray plus a little bit extra all round.

Mix up 700g (1lb 8½oz) resin with 200 drops of catalyst as before and apply over the gel coat with a brush. Do not use all the resin at this stage, just enough to make a thin layer.

Tray continued.

The quantity of materials given is generous for an average-sized tray, say, 60cm by 45cm (2ft by 1½ft). Chopped strand mat, about 1.8m (6ft), or just over four times the size of the tray. The mat is sold by weight so ask for a 300g weight (300g per square metre, or 1oz per sq ft).
Surfacing tissue, about 56cm (2ft approx.), or the size of the tray.
Rigid laminating resin with 10% thixotropic paste already added, about 1.8kg (4lb).
Resin pigment, about 28g (1oz).
Catalyst (hardener), comes in 56g (2oz) bottles. You will need most of this for a tray but follow manufacturer's instructions.
Emulsion wax release agent.
PVA (polyvinyl alcohol) release agent.
Metal polish.
Resin detergent or cleaner.
A mould such as a wooden, metal or plastic tray. The tray should be simply designed with no undercuts.
Varnish, such as polyurethane varnish. In this case include another 2.5cm (1in) paint brush.

1. *A homemade laminating roller.*
2. *Male and female moulds.*

3. *Using a wooden or plastic spatula ease the moulding away from the tray.*

4. *The new mould becomes the male mould from which the final tray is made.*

5. *Apply the wax release agent and polish to remove smears and unevenness.*

6. *Next, thoroughly cover the mould with polyvinyl release agent.*

7. *Pour a quantity of resin into a container and add the resin pigment.*

8. *Add the catalyst or hardener following the manufacturer's instructions.*

9. *Paint on the gel coat in a thin layer. This will hide the glass fibre.*

10. *Carefully place a layer of chopped strand mat over the gel coat.*

11. *Apply resin over the glass fibre and stipple into the mat with a brush.*

12. *Remove air bubbles by firmly rolling over with a laminating roller.*

13. *Surfacing tissue is the last layer and gives a good finish.*

14. *At gel stage cut off the superfluous glass fibre with a trimming knife.*

15. *The final trim: complete this stage immediately after the rough trim.*

16. *When the resin has set prise the two surfaces away with a spatula.*

17. *Separate the tray from the mould— the mould can be used again.*

18. *File down the edges of the tray and follow with silicon carbide paper.*

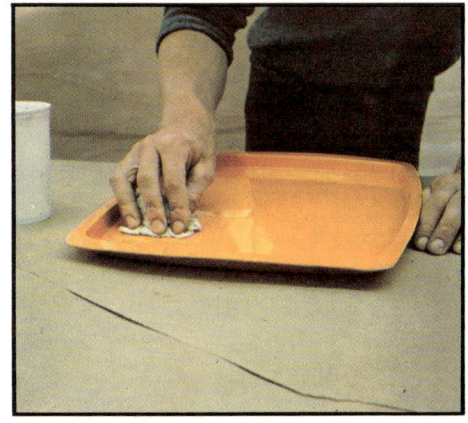

19. *Finish off by polishing with a metal polish for a good, shiny surface.*

20. *The finished tray: simple, strong, attractive and hard wearing.*

Carefully lay a piece of chopped strand mat on to the resin. The mat will easily stick to the resin. Apply more resin to the mat and work into the mat using the brush in a stippling (not brushing) action.

When the resin has been worked into the mat use the laminating roller to remove air pockets. Work from the middle of the tray to the outside. It is important to disperse all air pockets (which show as white patches) otherwise they may later burst and create small craters. Work right up to the edges of the mat.

Be particularly careful at corners. If necessary cut the mat and tease out the fibres until they meet. The corners may be initially stiff but will soften up when resin is applied.

Add another layer of mat and repeat the process until the glass fibre is thoroughly impregnated with resin. The intention is always to use the minimum amount of resin for the mat to be impregnated.

The last layer is the surfacing tissue to create a smooth surface over the rather rough chopped strand mat. Like the pigment this stage is not necessary when making a mould, but it gives a better finish for the final tray.

Wash the brush and roller in resin detergent and warm water. Allow to dry thoroughly.

When the mould starts to gel, trim the mat level with the side of the tray using a trimming knife. If you do not trim at this stage you will later have to do so with a hacksaw.

Allow the resin to set; this will take at least twenty four hours. A full cure takes about a week.

When the mould is cured it is time to separate the two components. Push a smooth, flat wooden or plastic spatula between the two edges (fig.3). Once air has been admitted the pieces will separate easily (fig.4). Don't use a metal tool as it may scratch the glass fibre. The remains of the polyvinyl alcohol will leave patches on the mould but this can easily be wiped clean.

When you have removed the shell from the mould you will have a tray but the top surface will be rough and the smooth side, with any pattern, will be underneath.

To produce your tray you have to repeat the whole process described above, using as a mould the glass fibre shell you have just made (figs.5 to 20). The only difference is that you will lay the fibre over the bottom or smooth side so that the final product has its smooth side uppermost.

Instead of adding pigment you can include a layer of thin, patterned cotton fibre. This looks very effective if you match a tray to curtains or a table cloth. Follow the directions for making the tray leaving out the pigment and placing the fabric between a very even front gel coat of resin and the layers of glass fibre so that the fabric design shows clearly. (Make sure the first layer of resin is a clear type.)

Even though the edges of the tray have been neatly trimmed with the knife you should still file them down and follow this with medium then fine silicon carbide paper.

Polish the finished surface of the tray with a metal polish.

Glass fibre lampshade

The technique applied to making a plastic tray by moulding resin-impregnated glass fibre over an already-existing tray can be used for any number of projects. All you need is a suitable mould and two basic raw materials: glass fibre cloth and laminating resin. When cured the glass fibre reproduces the exact shape of the mould. The lampshade shown here was made using a plastic mixing bowl. The mould could equally well make another bowl or even a hundred lampshades – one mould can make any number of objects. The lampshade is a simple curved shape embellished with embedded tissue and decorated with a scalloped edge and a fringe. Although it is made from an upturned bowl there is nothing clinical about it, it gives a soft, flowing light.

The lampshade was made from a bowl measuring 20cm (8in) in diameter. It is important to choose the right sort of mould, i.e. one with sloping sides (fig.1), otherwise you will find difficulty in separating the components.

Open the windows for good ventilation, lay down newspaper on the working surface, arrange all tools and materials, put on an apron and cover exposed skin with protective cream.

Wash and thoroughly dry the bowl. It is not necessary to make a mould from the mixing bowl.

Use the bowl as a female mould, i.e. the inside of the bowl is coated with glass fibre.

Polish the inside of the bowl with emulsion wax, followed by a coat of polyvinyl acetate (PVA) release agent (fig.2), following the instructions on page 113. Make absolutely sure you have completely covered the surface with release agent; this is coloured blue so you can see if you have left any bare patches.

Apply a thin layer of resin to the inside of the bowl. The thickness of the gel coat should be about 3mm ($\frac{1}{8}$in). Measure approximately 113g (4oz) of resin and add 9 to 10 drops of catalyst to each 28g (1oz). Follow manufacturer's instructions if in any doubt as to the quantity of catalyst needed. Paint a coat of activated resin on the inside of the bowl. The resin will tend to slip down towards the bottom of the bowl so push it up the sides with the brush.

Lampshade
You will need:
Tools as for making the tray, see page 112.
Hacksaw (optional).
Hand drill and small bit (optional).
Glass fibre is bought by the metre (yard) and you will need:
Chopped strand mat, 45cm (18in).
Surfacing tissue, 1m (3ft).
Rigid laminating resin with the addition of 10% thixotropic paste already mixed; about 0.5kg (1lb).
Catalyst (hardener) comes in 56gm (2oz) bottles.
Emulsion wax release agent.
PVA (polyvinyl acetate) release agent.
Two or three sheets of tissue paper in various colours.
Resin detergent or cleaner.
Epoxy adhesive (optional).
Medium silicon carbide abrasive paper.
Metal polish.
Protective hand cream.
Fringing, about 90cm (3ft).
A low-heat light bulb, i.e. 40 watt. Alternatively, use a cold ray bulb which is designed to produce very little heat. An ordinary bulb will heat up the plastic too much.
Lamp fitting and lamp base.
Plastic mixing bowl for use as a mould.
Note: The bowl should not be used for food preparation having been in contact with GRP.
Newspaper.

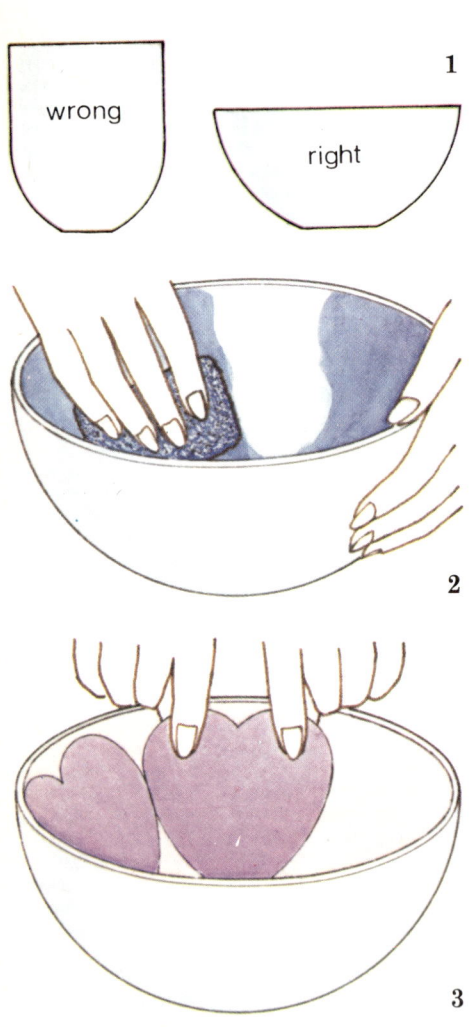

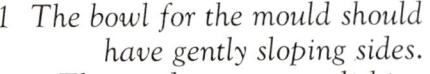

1 The bowl for the mould should
    have gently sloping sides.
2. The inside requires polishing
    with release agent.
3. After applying the fibre glass,
    add tissue paper decoration.

Wash out the brush in resin cleaner or detergent and leave resin
to gel for about an hour.

Make a paper pattern to fit the inside of the bowl. Cut out one sheet of chopped strand mat and two sheets of surfacing tissue equal to the area of the bowl plus a little over all the way round. Cut out tissue paper hearts or any other chosen shapes. When the resin has gelled carefully place most of the tissue shapes on to the resin, keeping the design simple and checking that there are no air bubbles trapped underneath (fig.3).

Mix up the rest of the resin with catalyst and apply a thin coat of resin over the paper shapes taking care not to disturb them.

Lay on the first layer of surfacing tissue and with the brush stipple the glass fibre into the resin to remove air bubbles and ensure that it is thoroughly impregnated with resin.

Place more paper shapes if needed to complete the design.

Paint on another layer of resin and lay the chopped strand mat on top of this, stippling the mat into the resin with the brush.

The final layer is surfacing tissue which is stippled into the resin as before. Paint on another coat of resin if needed otherwise use as little resin as is necessary to impregnate the glass fibre.

Wash out the brush in cleaner or resin detergent.

When the resin gels trim the edges of the glass fibre with a trimming knife.

Leave the lampshade overnight and then the shade should pull out of the mould with ease. If it does not then place the mould in hot

Far left: The completed lampshade can be adapted to a variety of lampstands by the addition of a suitable fringe.
Left: Trays may be decorated to match curtains or tablecloths by using material of the same type.

119

water followed by cold water.

Smooth the edge of the lampshade with abrasive paper. If making a lampshade with a scalloped edge cut out the curves with a hacksaw. Although the lampshade is quite safe to use with a low-wattage bulb you may like to drill three or four small holes in the top of the lampshade to let the heat escape. Use a hand drill and bit for this.

Polish the outside of the lampshade with a metal polish. Finally stick fringing round the edge with an epoxy adhesive. The lampshade can be placed over a table lampstand and lit by a low-heat bulb.

Glass fibre screen

A screen can be simply made from two layers of impregnated glass fibre. The result is thin, lightweight, quite strong, either coloured or water-clear and embedded, if you wish, with dried leaves, ferns, flowers or feathers; alternatively, try cut-out paper shapes or strips of material.

The screen will transmit light and is decorative as well as practical. It can be used for a bathroom window, in front of a light source, or as a shower screen.

Open the window to ventilate the room, put on an apron or overall and cover exposed areas of the skin with protective cream. Use a flat, smooth tabletop or working surface at least 1.2m by 0.75m (4ft by 2ft 6in) in area.

Cut a piece of cellophane or plastic sheet 1.2m by 0.75m (4ft by 2ft 6in) plus a little extra all the way round. If a join is necessary overlap the edges by 2.5cm (1in) tape all along the join with adhesive tape and turn over.

If you are using cellophane, dampen with water and stretch over the working surface. Tape in place using adhesive tape (fig.1). Do not crease the sheet unless you want a crinkled surface to the screen. When the cellophane dries it will stretch very tight and flat and will easily peel off the screen.

Measure out 0.67kg (1½lb) resin. Mix with catalyst which is generally used in the proportion of ten drops of catalyst per 28g (1oz); with largish quantities of resin such as are needed for the screen reduce the proportion of catalyst to around eight to nine drops per 28g (1oz).

Gently pour the activated resin on to the cellophane and evenly brush it over the surface with a laminating brush or paint brush. Alternatively, spread the resin with a strip of cardboard. Make sure that the resin extends a little outside the area of the screen. Wash out the brush with resin detergent or cleaner and allow the

---

Screen

You will need:
Tools. See page 112.
Strip of cardboard about 1.25m by 5cm (5in by 2in).
Glass fibre is bought by the metre (or yard) and you will need:
Surfacing tissue, 2.7m (9ft).
Chopped strand mat, either a small piece or one or two scraps for shaking over the screen.
Rigid laminating resin, 2.5kg (5½lb).
Catalyst (hardener). You will need most of a 56g (2oz) bottle.
Resin pigment (optional).
Dried ferns, leaves, flowers, or feathers for embedding.
Cellophane or plastic sheet just over twice the size of the screen.
Masking tape or other adhesive tape.
Flat board the size of the screen and weights (or heavy books) to press it down.
Resin detergent or cleaner.
Silicon carbide abrasive paper.
Metal polish.
Protective hand cream.
Large apron or overall.
Newspaper.

Left: An attractive screen for the bathroom made by sandwiching peacock feathers between two layers of glass fibre.

resin to gel for about an hour.

Mix up 225g (½lb) resin with a small quantity of resin pigment (if used). Add catalyst and pour evenly over the gel coat. Spread out with the card.

At this stage arrange the leaves, ferns or feathers to your design. Place them face downwards. By sitting the objects in a 'puddle' of resin, bubbles of air are discouraged from forming around them (fig.2). Alternatively, wait until this layer has gelled before placing the objects on top. This method will encourage bubbles which can look very attractive in this type of screen. (You will probably get a few bubbles anyway.)

When the resin has gelled cut a layer of surfacing tissue equal to the size of the screen plus a little extra all the way round. Gently place over the objects.

Mix up another 225g (½lb) resin with catalyst and apply to the gelled coat, thoroughly stippling it into the surfacing tissue being careful to completely cover the objects. Allow the resin to gel and trim with a trimming knife. Do not leave this to a later stage when you will have to trim with a hacksaw.

Allow this half of the screen to harden overnight, remove from the working surface and place on a flat surface nearby.

Mix up 0.67kg (1½lb) resin with catalyst as before and spread over a fresh sheet of cellophane in an even layer. Allow to gel.

Mix up 225g (½lb) resin with resin pigments (if used) and apply to the outer edge of the second layer to make a border. Leave the centre clear as far as possible. Allow to gel. Hold a piece of chopped strand mat over the screen and shake vigorously so that separate strands of glass fibre fall on to the screen. These will increase the strength of the screen and are practically invisible.

Cut a layer of surfacing tissue equal to the area of the screen plus a little extra. Place over the gelled resin.

Mix up 0.45kg (1lb) resin with catalyst. Leave this resin clear. Impregnate the surface tissue, stippling it in thoroughly. Also coat the back of the first layer of the screen with resin.

Carefully lay the first layer wet side down on top of the new side. It will be possible to slide the top part a few inches to adjust but, if you do, take it slowly and gently and do not try to lift it off. Using a trimming knife trim the bottom layer flush with the top using the top edges as a guide. Place a flat board on top of the screen and weight it down. Leave to set overnight.

If you are fixing the screen into a frame there will be no need to smooth down the edges (fig.3). If they do need smoothing rub with wet silicon carbide abrasive paper. Leave the cellophane for as long as you can and then peel off. Polish with a metal polish.

1. Stretch damp cellophane.
2. The feathers in position.
3. The screen is framed.

Working with acrylics

Acrylic sheeting is probably better known by various trade names such as Perspex or Plexiglass. It is a thermoplastic which means that it becomes pliable when heated and can therefore be used for moulding and bending. It also has excellent clarity and can transmit 92% of light.

Acrylic is an extremely versatile material to work with – it can be dissolved with solvents such as chloroform, stuck together, cut, drilled and moulded to produce a wide range of useful and attractive objects. Ordinary wood-working or metal-working tools can be used for cutting acrylic although it does tend to blunt saws and files rather quickly. Special glues are needed for sticking acrylic as many types of glue attack the plastic or will not adhere.

Below: Acrylic offcuts like these may be bought quite cheaply.

Acrylic comes in a variety of different forms: it can be bought in sheets, tubes, rods and blocks, and it is also possible to buy bags of offcuts which are cheaper and ideal for craft work. It is available in a wide range of colours; all colours of the rainbow in both clear and opaque, as well as black and white, luminous colours, and some special types such as mother-of-pearl. It is also possible to obtain special types with patterned surfaces.

Acrylic is a rather brittle substance and can become scratched or broken if not worked with sufficient care. When you buy sheeting it will be covered with protective adhesive paper. This paper should be kept on the acrylic during sawing and drilling, in fact until the last possible moment to prevent the surface becoming damaged.

Letter rack

This letter rack is very simply constructed from a series of different coloured rectangles. It is 14cm by 10cm (5in by 4in) and 14.3cm ($5\frac{5}{8}$in) high.

Leaving the protective paper on the acrylic, mark out rectangles using pencil, ruler and set square to get right-angled corners.

Secure the sheet to the working surface with a G-cramp, using a piece of wood under the foot of the cramp to spread the load over a greater area (fig.1).

Using a mechanical saw or hacksaw, saw the sheet. Cut slightly outside the line to allow for finishing afterwards. Be very careful not to chip or crack the acrylic during sawing. This can be avoided by securing firmly and sawing slowly and smoothly. Any great strain put on the acrylic by jerking or forcing the saw through it may cause chipping or crazing. If you are using a mechanical saw, beware of sawing too quickly. Heat generated by friction will melt the plastic which will then join up again after the saw has passed through it.

Once you have cut one side of the rectangle move the acrylic into position for sawing the next edge.

When all the pieces of the letter holder have been cut out, the edges must be 'finished'.

Using a wood file, file down edges to pencil line until they are as smooth as possible. The edges which glue to the base must be straight and square to the surface.

One 10cm (4in) edge of each of the uprights (i.e. the edge to be glued to the base) can be left unfinished. All other edges and the four edges of the base need further work.

Place the medium silicon carbide paper on a flat surface and put a few drops of water in the centre of the paper. Rub the edges of

Letter rack

You will need:
Acrylic sheet 3mm ($\frac{1}{8}$in) thick in the following colours and sizes:
Yellow 14cm by 10cm ($5\frac{1}{2}$in by 4in).
Orange 11.5cm by 10cm ($4\frac{1}{2}$in by 4in).
Red 9cm by 10cm ($3\frac{1}{2}$in by 4in).
Dark red 6.5cm by 10cm ($2\frac{1}{2}$in by 4in).
Red 13.2cm by 10cm (5in by 4in) for base.
Hacksaw or mechanical saw such as a Black and Decker (one with a fine-toothed blade).
Medium-sized wood file.
G-cramp.
Sharp knife or scalpel.
Silicon carbide paper, medium and fine.
Soft cloth for polishing.
Thin stick such as an orange stick.
Metal polish.
Acrylic glue.
Pencil and ruler, set square.

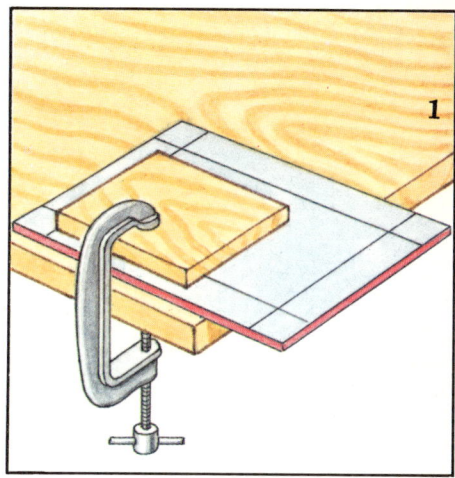

Left: The finished letter rack.
1. When cramping the acrylic sheet, it is important to use a block of scrap wood to spread the load imposed by the foot of the cramp.

the acrylic rectangles on the silicon carbide paper in a circular motion, making sure that the cut edge is placed flat on the surface of the paper (fig.2). Repeat with fine silicon carbide paper.

Leave matt or, using a soft cloth, metal polish and lots of elbow grease, rub the edges until they are as smooth and shiny as possible. The acrylic pieces can now be stuck together to make a letter rack. Using a pencil and ruler mark out the position of the four uprights on to the base (fig.3). With a sharp knife cut the paper along the pencil lines but do not damage the acrylic underneath. Peel off the strips of paper (fig.4).

Paint some glue along strip A and along edge B (fig.5) with a thin stick. Using a set square to make sure you are holding the upright at right angles to the base, put the two glued surfaces together and hold for a minute (fig.6).

Repeat the process for the other three uprights making sure that

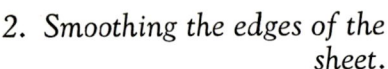

2. Smoothing the edges of the sheet.

3. The position of the uprights on the base.

4. Peel off strips to expose the acrylic for glueing.

5. Glue is applied sparingly and the two edges are brought together.

6. Make sure that the joints are square before proceeding further.

7. The order of the uprights on the base.

2

3

4cm(1½") 3mm(⅛")

4cm(1½")

4cm(1½") 3mm(⅛")

4

5

6.5cm(2½")

A

B

6

7

6.5cm(2½")

9cm (3½")

11.5cm (4½")

14cm (5½")

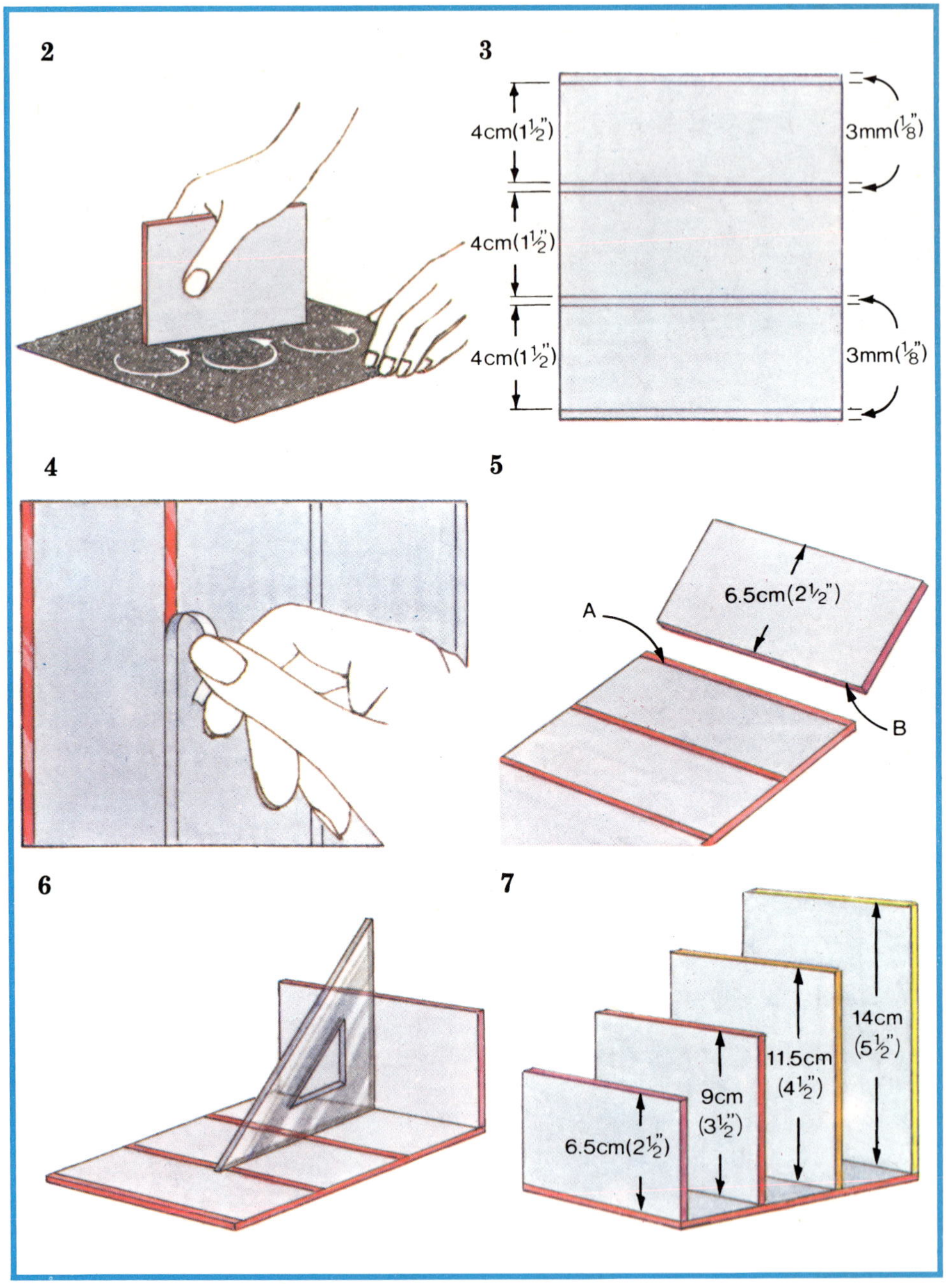

they are in the right order (fig.7).

Although it takes some time to reach full strength, acrylic glue sets very quickly so you have to work fast. Beware of putting on too much glue.

When you have finished gluing, peel off the rest of the protective paper and your letter rack is complete.

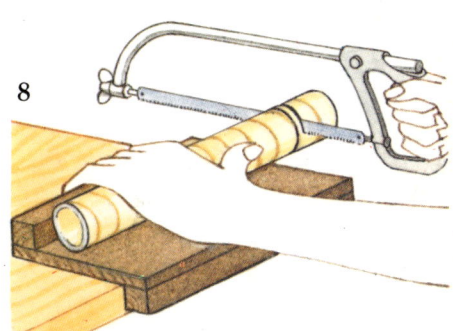

8

Left: A simply made pencil holder.
8. Wedge tube in L-shape for cutting.

Pencil holder

You will need :
Tools, as for letter rack and masking tape.
Bench hook or other L-shape to wedge tube against during sawing.
Acrylic sheet 3mm ($\frac{1}{8}$in) thick, 15cm by 15cm (6$\frac{1}{4}$in by 6$\frac{1}{4}$in) for base.
Acrylic tubing in the following sizes :
Two 6cm (2$\frac{1}{2}$in) outside diameter, 8cm (3in) long.
One 5cm (2in) outside diameter, 13cm (5in) long.
One 3.8cm (1$\frac{1}{2}$in) outside diameter, 4cm (1$\frac{3}{4}$in) long.

Pencil holder

The pencil holder is about 15cm (6$\frac{1}{4}$in) square and 13cm (5in) high. As acrylic tubing does not come with protective paper, you must first of all wrap outer surfaces with masking tape. If you have not bought the tubing cut to the required lengths, follow these instructions for cutting the tubes.

Using a pencil and ruler, mark off the required lengths on tubes. Wedge tube against bench hook and saw through tube (fig.8). Saw just outside the line to allow for finishing. Once you have cut through the thickness of the tube wall, start to turn the tube towards you as you saw, so that you are cutting one rather than two thicknesses at the same time.

Cut base as for letter holder and finish off cut ends as for letter holder. Only one end of each tube and the four sides of the base need polishing.

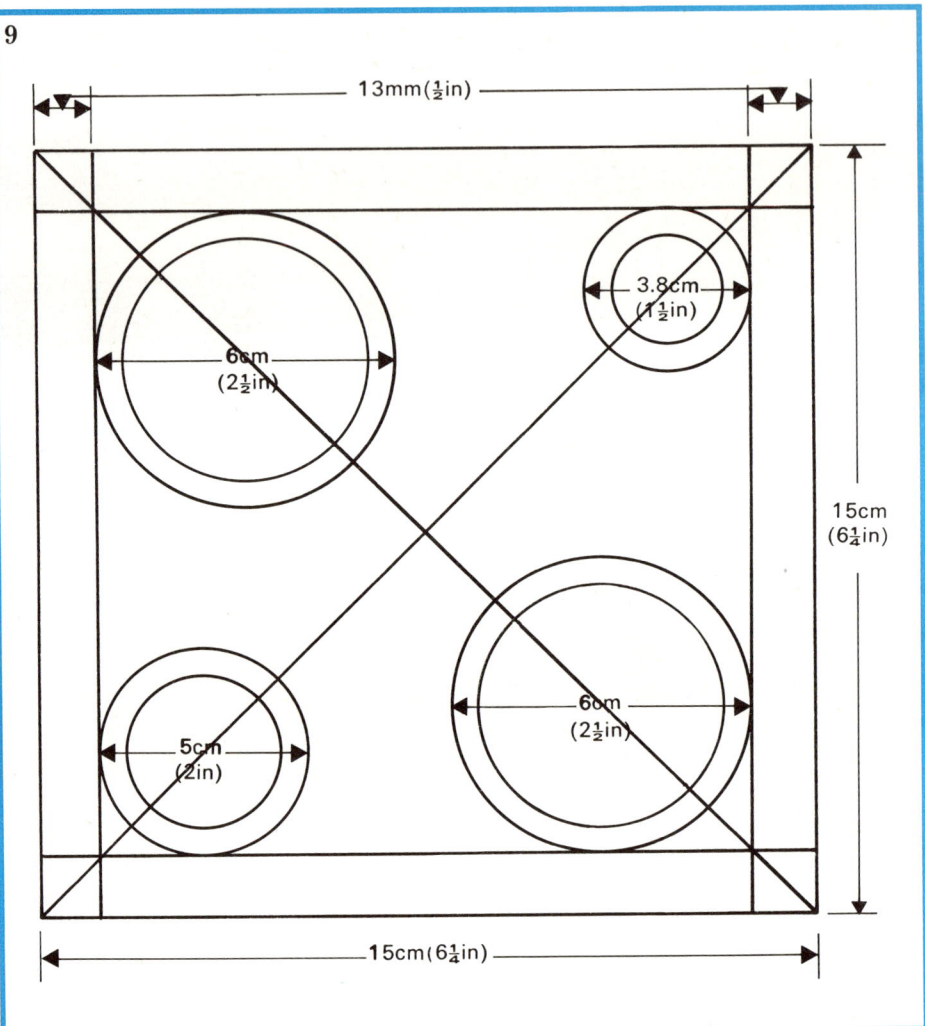

13mm(½in)

3.8cm (1½in)

6cm (2½in)

15cm (6¼in)

5cm (2in)

6cm (2½in)

15cm(6¼in)

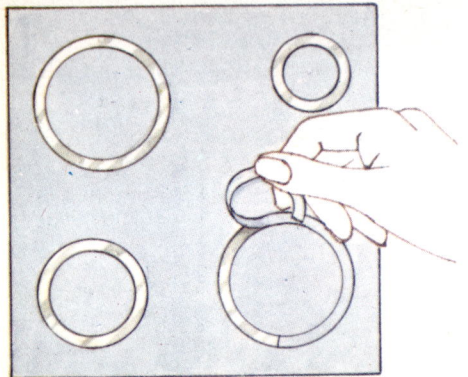

9. *The positions for the tubes are marked on the base while the paper surfacing is still intact.*
10. *Remove the protective coating and apply glue to the exposed acrylic.*

Using a set square check to see that the sides of the tube make a right angle with the base. If the tube does not stand up straight, sand down where necessary.

Draw the outlines of the tubes by placing tube in position and drawing round the inside and outside edges on to the base.

Cut along pencil lines and peel off paper (fig.10) as for the letter rack.

Apply glue to unpolished end of tube and to the corresponding location on base. Peel off paper inside circle. Put the two surfaces together and hold firmly for a minute. Stick the other three tubes in the same way.

Peel off protective paper and masking tape when glue is completely dry.

Expanded polystyrene

Expanded polystyrene (otherwise known as EPS) sheets and tiles are easy to work, readily available from wallpaper and hardware shops and inexpensive to buy.

The sheets or tiles are easily cut to any shape you wish. The shapes can be used for theatrical props, for Christman decorations and other festivities, for mobiles or to hang on a wall.

Below: A colourful sun easily made using expanded polystyrene tiles.

A sun

Using the compasses or a plate, draw a circle on tracing paper.

Mark off radii at 30° intervals along the perimeter (fig.1). On a spare piece of tracing paper experiment with the 'rays' of the sun by drawing round part of the edge of a saucer or glass for the top rounded part of the ray then move the saucer and draw again for the underside of the ray (fig.2). The base of the ray must be the same width as the 30° intervals marked on the perimeter of the circle. When you have made a satisfactory shape, cut round it and place it in position between two radii, then tape down and draw round. Repeat all the way round the circle (fig.3); this makes the pattern.

Tape the tracing paper tightly over the EPS. Using the ruler to keep the knife steady cut through the paper and the EPS at the same time. Stick the paper down with small tabs of tape as you go. Cut steadily and carefully; the knife may otherwise go off at a tangent.

To make the centre disc, draw a circle on to the tracing paper with radius equal to three quarters of the radius used for the first circle.

Tape tracing paper over another EPS sheet and cut out disc.

Position disc in centre of sun and glue on with a few specks of adhesive.

A sun

You will need:
Two square sheets of EPS (expanded polystyrene) any size you wish for sun and any depth up to about 13mm ($\frac{1}{2}$in). Buy type FRA (Flame Retardant Additive).
Tracing paper the same size as the EPS.
Spare piece of tracing paper.
Masking tape or other adhesive tape.
Sharp knife (or scissors for children).
Metal or plastic ruler, protractor.
Pencil, felt-tip pen, pair of compasses, plate, saucer or glass.
PVA adhesive.

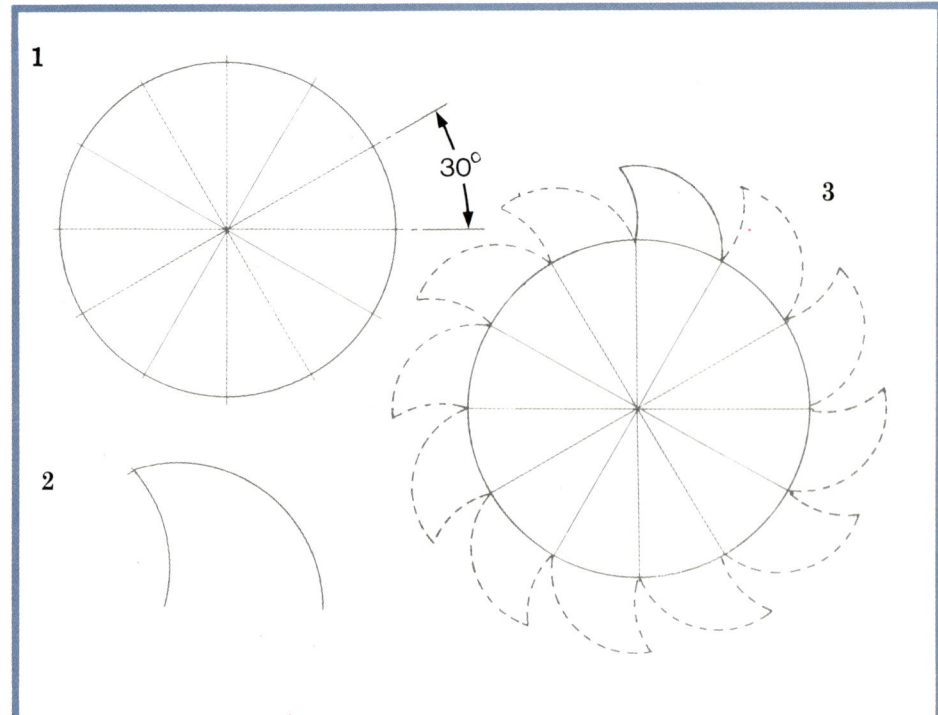

1. The first stage in marking out the sun.
2. One ray is made by joining the arcs of a circle.
3. The rays drawn on to the circle.

A letter

An alphabet letter can be cut from EPS using the same technique as for the sun.

Start with the letter R shown here or any other letter of your choice. Choose a simply shaped letter to begin with and do not start making complicated letters until you have had a little practice. Practise on a scrap piece of paper before transferring to tracing paper.

Draw the rounded inner curve of the R first. To do this take a glass or saucer of suitable size and draw half way round it to make a semi-circle. Extend arms of curve in two straight parallel lines. Draw the outer side of the curve, making it an equal distance away from the inner curve. Draw in dots first, then connect to make a smooth curve. Look at the photograph to judge how far to extend the lines. Draw the straight upright lines.

A letter
You will need : Tools and materials the same as for the sun.

Left: Again from expanded polystyrene tiles; a letter of the alphabet.

If you wish to make a slightly smaller letter, make a template first from the original letter then cut the tracing paper R down by a small amount all round. Use this to cut out a smaller letter.

If you want to make a slightly larger letter tape the tracing paper R to more tracing paper and draw another letter slightly larger than the first, using the original letter as a guide.

Tape the tracing paper over the EPS. The two sizes of letter can be stuck together using a PVA adhesive.

A contour map

Older children, under supervision, will enjoy a project which shows their town or village in its surroundings.

It is quite a simple process to cut and stick EPS tiles to make a contour map. First locate your area on the map, choose an area not more than 4km square (2 square miles).

Draw the square on a scrap piece of tracing paper. Mark off along the edges of the square at 6mm ($\frac{1}{4}$in) intervals, and lightly connect the marks to make a grid. Place the square over your chosen area on the map and firmly tape down.

Trace in the major contours first, then draw the intermediate contours. Mark each contour in a different colour for identification (fig.4).

Number the different contours starting at 0 for the lowest contour. This will later help you to construct the model.

To enlarge the map mark a 61cm by 61cm (2ft by 2ft) board or cardboard into the same number of squares as the traced map. Then, working section by section, transfer the contour lines on the traced map to the board (see 'Enlarging and reducing designs' page 6).

Make a separate tracing of each contour line on a different sheet of tracing paper and number each tracing with the number of the contour line.

Place tracing of contour 0 over EPS tile and tape down making

<table>
<tr><td colspan="2">

Contour map

</td></tr>
<tr><td colspan="2">

You will need:
Contour map of the area such as survey map about 2cm to a kilo-metre (1in to a mile) in scale.
White board or stiff cardboard 61cm by 61cm (2ft by 2ft).
EPS tiles about 6mm ($\frac{1}{4}$in) thick and 61cm (2ft) square. Buy 10 to 12 tiles, type FRA; the exact number of tiles needed will depend on the height of the land and how many contour lines you choose to show. The contour map illustrated here uses 11 tiles.
11 sheets of tracing paper the same size as the board.
Scrap of tracing paper.
Masking tape or clear adhesive tape.
PVA adhesive.
Sharp knife (or scissors for children).
Metal or plastic ruler, preferably 61cm (2ft) long although a smaller ruler will be adequate.
Pencil and felt-tip pen.

</td></tr>
</table>

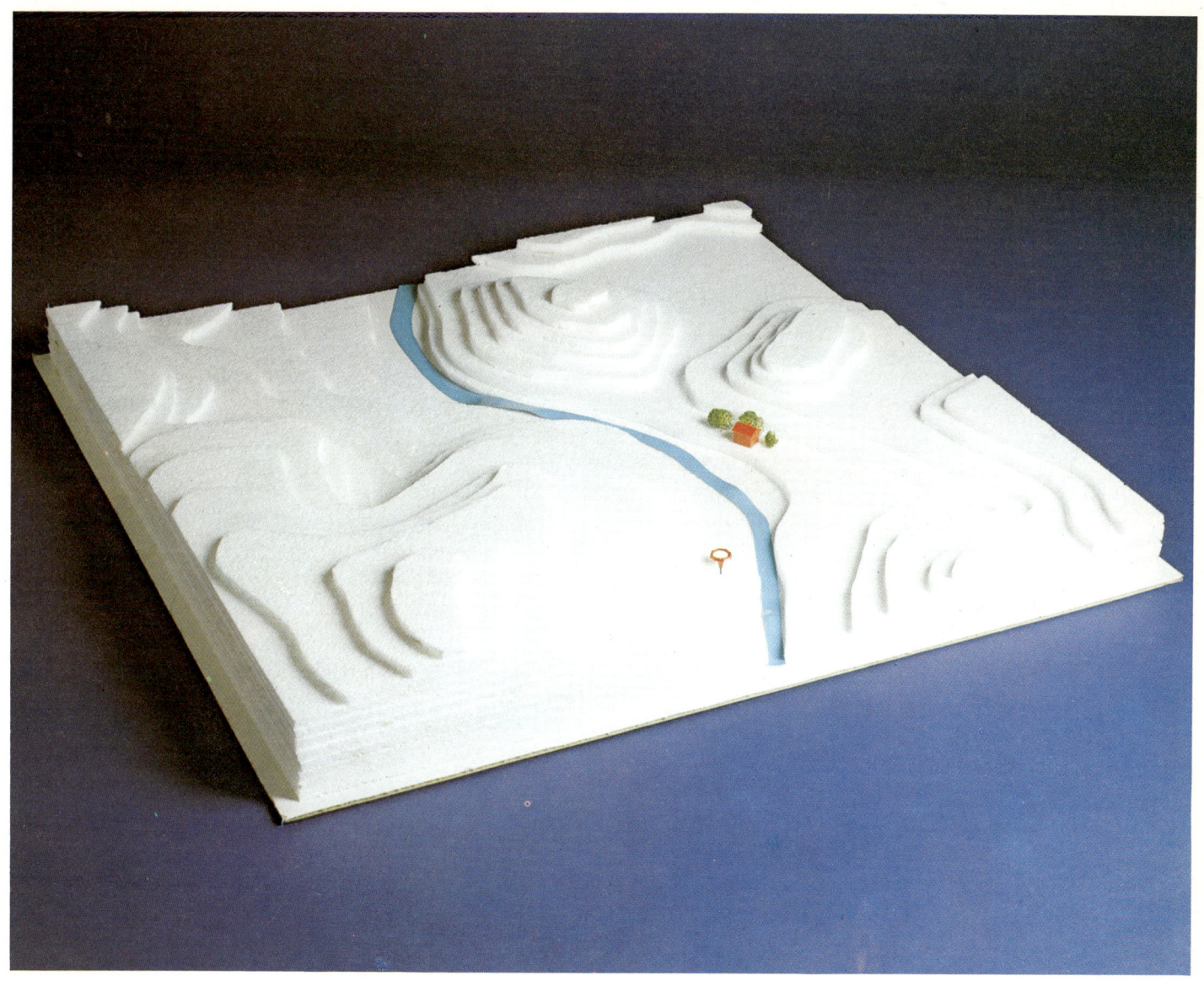

sure the edges are lined up. Cut along contour line. Cut through the tracing paper and the EPS at the same time using a scalpel or trimming knife. You have now cut out area 0 (fig.5) and are left with areas 1 to 10 still to cut.

Place the next piece of tracing paper over another tile and tape down. Cut along the contour line marked 1 in the same way as before. You have now cut out area 1 (fig.6) and are left with area 2. Mark the back of the tile with the appropriate number. Repeat this process and cut out each contour from a fresh EPS tile numbering the back as you go along.

Left and above: Two views of the contour map described here. The final detail is a matter of personal choice.

Stick together all the cut-out pieces with PVA adhesive. Look at the map as a guide and start from the highest number down, i.e. 10 is glued to 9, 9 to 8 and so on until you reach 0. Finally, glue the last tile to the board or cardboard.

Only spots of adhesive are needed for gluing.

The model may either be left as it is or water-based paints used to make it look as realistic as possible.

As a final touch add tiny buildings (bought from a toy shop or made from cardboard); trees, roads and any other details of the landscape can also be shown depending on how far you want to go with the finish.

Decorative finishes

You can leave EPS as it is but it will last longer if you apply one or more decorative finishes.

Any rough edges should first be smoothed with a fine grade glass-paper.

For painting, mix up the paints to the consistency of single cream and apply two coats of pale emulsion before finishing off with the final coat of paint of your choice. Finish by varnishing.

Alternatively, glaze EPS by using a little PVA adhesive mixed with water.

When dyeing, first seal the beads by painting them with a thin coat of emulsion.

Mix up a small quantity of PVA adhesive with a little water to thin it. Mix a little dye with the adhesive until you get the right shade (it will appear darker than the finished result).

'Paint' with dye. The PVA adhesive will give a good glaze to the dye. Polish with a soft cloth.

Another alternative is to mix in inks or food colouring with the adhesive.

Metallic finish EPS can look most attractive if it is painted first with a dark coloured paint such as dark green and then given a metallic finish.

Dip a soft cloth into wax such as shoe polish and, using only a small amount, dip again into gold or copper powder.

Buff across the EPS surface.

Allow the wax to harden for two days.

A great deal of fun can be had finishing expanded polystyrene models of this kind. The beauty of the material is that it is inexpensive so you can experiment with different finishes until you find one that suits the particular projects you are working on. It is probably worthwhile to use a couple of tiles and try out different effects on them.

Decorative finishes

You will need:
Paints; these must be water-based, such as poster paints, emulsion paints or gouache colours if they are not to dissolve the surface of EPS.
Water-based dyes or water-based inks or food colouring.
PVA adhesive; this is mixed with the dye to give a translucent glaze.
PVA varnish to coat the surface of painted EPS.
Gold or copper powder.
Wax such as furniture polish or tan shoe polish for use with the gold and copper powder.
Paint brushes.
Soft cloth.

Glossary

Acrylic A thermoplastic, better known by various trade names such as Perspex or Plexiglass. It can be disolved with solvents, stuck together, cut, drilled and moulded. It transmits 92 % of light.

Antique glass Traditional stained or coloured glass. The colour is obtained from metal oxides added to glass at molten stage.

Calme Length of leading produced in a variety of widths and thicknesses.

Embedding Process whereby an object is surrounded by a solid mass of resin.

Engraving A technique of cutting into a hard surface, i.e. glass.

Etching Technique of allowing controlled amounts of acid to eat away selected parts of a surface to make a design.

Filler A material used to give a cast weight to cut down on the amount of resin used, or to give it a metallic appearance.

Glass cullet Broken glass sold by weight as off-cuts by most glass merchants.

Mosaic work The craft of making designs and pictures by embedding small stones into a surface.

Plastic Collective word for a number of lightweight materials. Made up of chemicals derived from coal and petroleum.

Point work A method of engraving glass with a diamond or steel point, either by the drawing of fine lines into the surface or the creation of thousands of fine dots.

Polyester resin A liquid which solidifies by a chemical reaction when a catalyst is added.

Pour Term used for a layer in the embedding process.

Radius cutter Special tool used for cutting circles or semi-circles in glass.

Smalti Coloured glass cut into squares and used in mosaics. Gold smalti, made in Ravenna, were used in Christian mosaics.

Stained glass Term most popularly used to describe Antique glass. True stained glass is made by painting the glass with a gum resin, subsequently fired to give a yellow stain.

Stippling Engraving technique that creates thousands of fine dots on the surface of the glass.

Templates Cardboard patterns used in making glass objects such as a lampshade.

Terrarium A mini-greenhouse.

Tesserae Small cubes or squares of glass used in mosaic work.

Thermoplastics Plastics which are hard at normal temperature but soften when heated.

Thermosetting plastics Plastics that solidify in the presence of heat and once shaped and cooled, they cannot be reworked.

Wheel engraving The grinding into the surface of a piece of glass using small copper discs and an abrasive cutting agent such as Carborundum grit.

Index